EDITOR: LEE JOHNSON

OSPREY MILITARY

ELITE SERIES

53

THE INTERNATIONAL BRIGADES IN SPAIN 1936-39

Text by
KEN BRADLEY
Colour plates by
MIKE CHAPPELL

D1245661

First published in Great Britain in 1994 by
Osprey, an imprint of Reed Consumer Books Ltd.
Michelin House, 81 Fulham Road,
London SW3 6RB
and Auckland, Melbourne, Singapore and Toronto

ISBN 1 85532 367 2

Filmset in Great Britain
Printed through Bookbuilders Ltd, Hong Kong

Author's dedication
To the volunteers of the International Brigades who
gave all they had to oppose international fascism and to
preserve a free Spain.

Author's acknowledgements
I would like to express my sincere thanks to the fol-
lowing for their assistance in the preparation of this
work:
The Marx Memorial Library (which supplied photos
from the International Brigade Memorial Archive); the
International Brigade Association; Bill Alexander, Max
Colin, Tony Atienza, Tish Newland, Gabriel Perez,
Paul Compton, David Payne; the staffs of the British
Library; Norwich City College Library and
Reprographic Unit; and to the many authors (some of
whom are ex-International Brigaders) whose books I
have consulted and found useful (see Select
Bibliography). Also to Margaret, Richard and Gordon
for their support, and to many others too numerous to
mention. Photographs are reproduced by kind permis-
sion of: The Marx Memorial Library/International
Brigade Memorial Archive (IBMA). Copyright
International Brigade Memorial Archive at the Marx
Memorial Library, 37A Clerkenwell Green, London,
EC1R 0DU (tel: 071 253 1485); the International
Brigade Association (IBA); 'Book of the 15th Brigade'
(BFB); and Bill Alexander (BA).

Editor's note
In order to maintain consistency with MAA 74 *The
Spanish Civil War 1936–39*, the terms 'Nationalist' and
'Republican' are used in this book to describe the two
sides. The International Brigaders themselves referred
to their Nationalist enemies as 'Fascists', and to the
Spanish Civil War itself as the 'Spanish Anti-Fascist
War'. For clarity, Arabic numerals are used throughout
for battalions, brigades, divisions and corps, in place of
the Roman numerals in use at the time.

The editors wish to express their thanks to Dave
Ryan and Martin Windrow for their help in producing
this book.

For a catalogue of all books published by Osprey Military
please write to:

**The Marketing Manager,
Consumer Catalogue Department,
Osprey Publishing Ltd,
Michelin House, 81 Fulham Road,
London SW3 6RB**

THE INTERNATIONAL BRIGADES

BACKGROUND

The events leading up to the Spanish Civil War were very complex, but may be summed up by some simple statistics (quoted in the film *To Die in Madrid*). In 1931 Spain was a country of 24 million people, 12 million of them illiterate and 8 million poverty-stricken. Two million peasants owned no land; 20,000 people owned half of Spain, and entire provinces were owned by one man. The average worker's wage was one to three pesetas a day; a loaf of bread cost one to two pesetas. Spain had 31,000 priests, 20,000 monks, 60,000 nuns, and 5,000 convents. Her army had 15,000 officers (including 800 generals): i.e. one officer to every six men, and one general to every 100 men.

From 1923 to 1930 the Spanish government had been under the military dictator General Miguel Primo de Rivera. Against this background of poverty and backwardness, in June 1931 the people overwhelmingly elected a Republican government, with the Socialists holding the largest number of seats. King Alfonso XIII abdicated and went into exile. The people at last seemed to have hope of a way out of the medievalism which still dominated Spain. In Madrid they enthusiastically mobbed their newly elected leaders, and vented their rage by burning down several churches. A new constitution was drafted for the Second Spanish Republic, which pronounced that Spain was a 'democratic Republic of workers of all classes . . . Government emanated from the People and all citizens were equal . . . No titles of nobility would be recognised. Both sexes would vote at 23.' Under a 1932 agrarian reform law the unworked land in certain parts of Spain was to be redistributed to the peasants. Parts of Spain that felt themselves separate, such as the Catalan and Basque Republics, were to be given a degree of autonomy. The power of the church and army was curbed. It is hardly surprising that certain elements in Spain regarded these reforms as

The Tom Mann Centuria, Barcelona, 1936. Left to right: Sid Avner (later in Thaelmann Bn.); Nat Cohen (leader); Ramona Cohen; Tom Wintringham (later CO, British Bn.); George Tioli, an Italian living in Britain; Jack Barry (Australian); Dave Marshall (later in Thaelmann Bn.). Little military equipment is evident. Note Wintringham's alpargatos sandals, which were widely worn by all Spanish units including the International Brigades.The banner is reconstructed as our colour Plate K2. (IBMA)

dangerously threatening.

In August 1932 General José Sanjurjo Sacanell attempted a *pronunciamiento* (military coup) which the government easily suppressed. This rising led to strikes, with attendant violence and destruction. Following widespread dissatisfaction with the government (including the armed suppression of workers in Casas Viejas) the government resigned; and new elections in November 1933 led to a victory for a coalition of right-wing, traditionalist parties including the CEDA (a bourgeois Catholic party) and the Falange Español (the Fascist party), supported by various monarchist and other factions. These were to be the parties that supported the Nationalists in the Civil War. This right-wing government proceeded to reverse the reforms of the Socialist-dominated government of 1931–33: estates were restored, wages cut, peasants evicted, and Sanjurjo and his accomplices amnestied. Leading socialists like Francisco Largo Caballero ('the Spanish Lenin') were now arguing that revolution was the only answer to save Spain from fascism.

In October 1934 the left attempted an insurrection, but only in the mining area of Asturias did the rising have any effect. A 'Red Army' of 30,000 workers had been mobilised. Against this force the government sent Colonel Juan Yagué with units of the Spanish Foreign Legion and Moroccan *regulares*. These troops ruthlessly suppressed the rising, leaving 2,000 killed or wounded and 30,000 political prisoners.

Elections were held in February 1936, and to counter the right-wing National Front the parties of the left grouped together to form the Popular Front; this coalition achieved 268 seats to the National Front's 157, with centre parties holding 48. This Popular Front government in turn proceeded to reverse everything the right had done, and saw as its task the modernisation and democratisation of Spain. Some workers and peasants, disappointed at the inaction of previous governments, seized large tracts of land; more churches were burnt down; fascist gunmen toured the streets of major cities killing political opponents. This led to revenge killings by the left, and the spiral of violence grew ever more bitter.

In secret, right-wing army officers with support from monarchist and fascist elements planned a coup. The army was divided between the right-wing UME (Union Militar Española) and the left-wing UMRA (Union Militar Republicano Anti-Fascista). General Emilio Mola, in Pamplona, directed the plans of the UME; other generals (including Franco, Goded and Sanjurjo) and lesser

Poster issued by the International Brigades: 'The Internationals, united with the Spaniards, fight the invader' (artist: Parrilla). Note in background 'La Bonita Juanita' ('the beautiful girl', the symbol of the Second Spanish Republic) with background of Republican flag in red, yellow and purple; French helmet; and beret bearing the red three-pointed star of the International Brigades, not widely worn in practice as a badge; and clenched-fist salute of the Popular Front in cartouche in foreground. (IBA)

officers were also involved in the plot to overthrow the Popular Front government. Against a background of terrorism and general instability the UME moved against the government with a rising in Spanish Morocco on 18 July 1936 and simultaneous risings on the mainland. Approximately one half of the Peninsular Army of Spain went over to the fascists, including some of the most senior officers. After some hesitation the Popular Front government armed the people, organised in their trade union and party militias, to counter the fascist rising: the Spanish Civil War had begun.

The Republican government was able to count on some loyal officers and troops, but in mid-1936 more reliance was initially placed upon the trade union and party militias, together with loyal sections of the Guardia Asaltos, Guardia Civil and Carabineros, together with volunteer units of foreigners. The fascists had with them from the outset the Spanish Foreign Legion, the Moroccan *regulares*, rebel Peninsular Army contingents on the Spanish mainland, Carlist Requetes and fascist Blueshirt militia amongst other elements. The Army of Africa (Foreign Legionaries and Moroccans) were a disciplined force hardened in campaigns against Rif tribesmen, and had little compunction at rising against the government – unlike the Peninsular Army, which was divided in its loyalty roughly fifty–fifty.

From the outset, therefore, the 'Nationalists' brought in foreign troops, as the whole of the Peninsular Army could not be counted on. Nazi Germany soon aided them by sending aircraft to ferry troops from Africa to Spain; eventually the Condor Legion (mainly German air squadrons, with some tank and artillery elements) fought on the Nationalist side, as did several divisions of Italian troops (including fascist 'Blackshirt' militia formations), some Portuguese, and, more trivially, O'Duffy's 'Blueshirts' from Ireland. The Nationalists were better equipped and supplied by their allies than the Republican armies, but the Republicans too had international aid. Materially

the greater part came from the USSR; but many volunteers from overseas enlisted to fight for the Republic, and some foreign units were among the earliest militias, paving the way for the later International Brigades.

Early International units

At the time of the formation of Spanish party and trade union militias several groups of foreigners either joined these, or formed their own in close co-operation. Some of the first foreign volunteers were athletes and others who had come to Barcelona for the Workers' Olympiad, which was to have taken place 19–26 July 1936 in opposition to the Olympic Games held in Berlin (which Adolf Hitler used as a shop-window for Nazism). The rebellion forestalled the *Olympiad Popular* but some athletes marched at the head of a workers' militia column to the Zaragoza front. Table A outlines some of these early groups. These early units, formed for the most part before the International Brigades were established, fought mainly on the Aragon Front with Catalan militias, though some were employed on other fronts. The Tom Mann Centuria, for instance, fought in Majorca as well as in Aragon; some others, especially the French, fought on the Northern Front in the Basque country at Irun.

Most volunteers came from left-wing political backgrounds of varying shades (socialist, communist, anarchist or merely 'anti-fascist'). They gen-

Table A: Representative early International units

Unit	Main nationality	Later served in Int. Bde.
Grupo Rakosi	Hungarian	150th (Rakosi Bn.)
Tom Mann Centuria	British	Some 11th, some 15th
Centuria Gaston Sozzi	Italian	12th (Garibaldi Bn.)
Thaelmann Centuria	German/Austrian	11th & 12th (Thaelmann Bn.)
Grupo Edgar André	French/Belgian	11th & 14th (Commune de Paris Bn.)
Grupo Dombrowski	Polish, Hungarian, Yugoslav	11th, 12th, 13th & 150th (Dombrowski Bn.)
Compania Ludwig Warymski	Slavic	Dombrowski Bn.
Grupo Walery Wroblewski	Polish	Dombrowski Bn.

André Marty (Catalan/French, 1886-1956), Chief of the International Brigades and First Commissar, at the Albacete base. He had led the mutiny of the French Black Sea Fleet when the French government tried to use them on the side of the Interventionist armies against the Bolshevik government of the USSR in 1919, and was a member of the Comintern. Note the black beret worn by many in the International Brigades. Alongside Marty is Luigi Longo, shown here in the type of leather jacket popular with International Brigaders. (BFB)

erally named their military formations after heroes of the working-class movement or revolutionary events or dates.

By October 1936 the first of the International Brigades, the 11th, was formed, followed in November by the 12th. Some of the above groups formed the foundation of the International Brigades, which were to make their name as something of an élite in the defence of Madrid, and subsequently on nearly every battlefield of the war. Most 'Brigaders' would not have claimed this status, however, pointing out that they were only five brigades (or eight, if the 86th, 129th and

150th are included) out of a total of 225 brigades in the Republican People's Army.

RECRUITMENT & COMPOSITION

At the same time as the polarisation of left and right in Spain into the Popular Front and the National Front, other countries were experiencing similar changes and strains; activists of both left and right identified their causes with the overseas flagbearers of their political philosophies – the USSR, Germany and Italy respectively. These enmities, growing in the fertile soil of domestic economic and political problems, led to greater or lesser degrees of violent unrest.

Far-sighted people on the left saw the dangers of the rise of fascism and the possibility of its escalation into a wider conflict. Italy, Germany and Austria had already fallen to fascism; Nazis were rearming and had already seized the Rhineland without a serious response from the democratic powers. The rise of the National Front and the military rebellion in Spain (which included the fascist Falange Party) was seen by many as an attempt by the fascists to gain a foothold in that country. France was understandably concerned, as she had two fascist neighbours already; if Spain fell she would be encircled. To many of the volunteers of the left, going to Spain was a way of fighting fascist power before it got a foothold anywhere else in Europe.

In mid-September 1936 there was a meeting in the NKVD headquarters in the Lubianka in Moscow, where the idea of foreign volunteers joining the Spanish Republican Army was mooted; the idea is variously credited to Thorez, leader of the French Communist Party, to Rosenburg, the Soviet Ambassador to Spain, to Tom Wintringham of the Communist Party of Great Britain, or to Dimitrov, the Bulgarian head of the Communist International (the Comintern). As Nazi Germany and Fascist Italy were also showing interest with a view to practising their military theories on Spanish soil, Soviet generals, too, saw

Table B: Nationalities in the International Brigades

Nationality	Total	Killed	Wounded
French/Belgians	10,000	3,000	
German/Austrian	5,000	2,000	
Italian	3,354	600	2,000
US	2,800	900	
British	2,300	526	1,200
Canadian	1,000	?	?
Yugoslav	1,500	750?	300
Hungarian	1,000	?	?
Czechoslovak	1,500	?	?
Scandinavian (inc 500 Swedes)	1,000	?	?
Swiss	?	76	?
53 other nations	3,000	?	?
Total:	32,000	7,852?+	3,500+

NB: Various other estimates have been made; given the impossibility of confirmation, conservative estimates are deliberately quoted here.

Not all of these people were in Spain at the same time; one estimate states that at any one time a maximum of 18,000 International Brigaders were in Spain. Other nationalities are included in the above figures, e.g. the 'British' Battalion also included Irish, Cypriots, Australians, Egyptians, New Zealanders, Hong Kong and volunteers from other countries of the then British Empire; the Lincoln Bn. included Canadians, Cubans, Irish, Greeks, Cypriots, etc.

the Spanish war as a cause for concern. A Comintern delegation was sent to Spain to discuss the idea; after certain assurances the Spanish government agreed, and the Comintern started to organise a network to get foreign volunteers to Spain to join the International Brigades as part of the Spanish Republican Army.

Recruitment was mainly (though not exclusively) handled through the Communist Parties in various countries. Some recruiting offices were innocent-looking restaurants and hotels, since some countries had laws prohibiting their nation-

Maxim machine gun: many of those in the International Brigades were elderly M1910 Soviet models. In Spain they often had to be carried on the back; the two steel wheels of the carriage played havoc with the carrier's kidneys. (IBMA)

als from enlisting in foreign armies. In Britain, the Communist Party HQ in King Street, London, together with certain other addresses, co-ordinated recruitment for what was to become the British Battalion of the 15th International Brigade. Volunteers – many of whom had no interest in communism – enlisted at these centres, and were then sent on a 'day trip' to Paris, where they joined other volunteers to be transported to the French-Spanish frontier; they crossed the Pyrenees on foot, avoiding both French and Catalan frontier guards if at all possible. Many

Table C: The International Brigades 1936-39

Bde. no., name & date formed	Battalions(Overall strength where known)	Main nationalities
11th Int. Bde. 'Hans Beimler' later 'Thaelmann' 22 October 1936	1. Edgar André 2. Commune de Paris (later transferred to 14th Int. Bde.) 3. Dombrowski (later transferred to 12th, 150th and 13th Int. Bdes.)	German Franco-Belgian[1] Polish
12th Int. Bde. 'Garibaldi' 5 November 1936	1. Thaelmann (later transferred to 11th Int. Bde.) 2. Garibaldi (3,354) 3. Andre Marty (later transferred to 150th, 12th and 14th Int. Bdes.)	German[2] Italian Franco-Belgian
13th Int. Bde. 'Dombrowski' 2 December 1936	1. Louise Michel (later transferred to 14th Int. Bde.) 2. Tchapiaev (388) (later transferred to 129 Int. Bde.) 3. Henri Vuillemin (later transferred to 14th Int. Bde.) 4. Mickiewicz, Palafox	Franco-Belgian Balkan French Polish
14th Int. Bde. 'La Marseillaise' 2 December 1936	1. Nine Nations Bn. (later transferred to Commune de Paris Bn.) 2. Domingo Germinal 3. Henri Barbusse 4. Pierre Brachet 5. La Marseillaise	 Spanish Anarchist French French French (No. 1 Co. British)
15th Int. Bde. (English-speaking) 31 January 1937	1. Dimitrov (1,500?) (later transferred to 129th & 13th Int. Bdes.) 2. British (2,300) 3. Abraham Lincoln 4. George Washington (amalgamated: 2,800) 5. MacKenzie-Papineau (1,000), originally with Lincoln Battalion 6. Sixth of February (later transferred to 14th Int. Bde.) 7. 59th Spanish EP Bn.	Yugoslav British US US Canadian Franco-Belgian
86th Mixed Bde. 129th Int. Bde. 13 February 1938	20th Int. Bn., no. 2 Co. (later transferred to 15th Int. Bde.) 1. Mazaryck (1,500) (attached 45th Division) 2. Dajakovich 3. Dimitrov (1,500) (originally with 15th, later 13th Int. Bde.) 35th Bty., 4th Arty. Gp.	British, US, Irish Czechoslovak Bulgarian Bulgarian, Yugoslav & Albanian British, US
150th Int. Bde. 27 May 1937	1. Rakosi (1,000?) 2. (later transferred to 13th Int. Bde.) 3. ?	Hungarian ?

NOTE: The transfers referred to above were an attempt to group the Brigades into nationalities to make communications less difficult. The brigade numbering is that of the Spanish Popular Army of which the International Brigades were a part: e.g. the British, Lincoln and MacPap Battalions were the 57th, 58th and 60th Bns., 15 Bde., 35th Division. Battalion numbers are listed in full in Table D. In 1938 the International Brigades in fact contained a majority of Spanish troops with the addition of Spanish companies and commanders.

[1] No. 4 Section of the MG Co. were British; survivors were transferred to the British Bn., 15th Int. Bde.

[2] No. 3 Section of No. 1 Co. were British; survivors were transferred to the British Bn., 15th Int. Bde.

made it, though some ended up briefly in internment. The successful ones were taken initially to Figueras Castle, a clearing station, and went from there by rail to Albacete, which had been assigned as the International Brigade base in autumn 1936.

Between 30,000 and 40,000 people from almost every country were eventually to join the International Brigades (see Table B). Some of the first to go were some 500 to 600 men exiled in the USSR from their own countries for their revolutionary activities. These were to fill the ranks of the very first International Brigade battalions (the 'Edgar André', 'Commune de Paris' and 'Dombrowski' Battalions) and were to distinguish themselves in the defence of Madrid in November 1936; they were Germans, French, Belgians, Poles, Hungarians, some British and a little later Italians. This was a politically committed volunteer force, fighting for its ideals, and not for money. Most were ordinary working-class people, with a smattering of intellectuals. Many had worked in the labour and trade union movements in their own countries. There were a few with other motives, but they were a small minority.

Eventually these volunteers were organised at or near Albacete into battalions and brigades. The 40-odd battalions of the International Brigades are listed on page 31. Not all these battalions were active at any one time, and several mergers took place as indicated. Some battalions existed only for a short period: the George Washington Battalion, for example, suffered so many losses at the battle of Brunete that it had to be merged with the Abraham Lincoln Battalion.

Each battalion was assigned to one of the five main International Brigades (the 11th to 15th) of the Spanish Popular Army, though some International battalions ended up in the 86th, 129th and 150th Brigades. Table C shows the initial organisation of the International Brigades. A reorganisation took place later in an attempt to group nationalities together to overcome language difficulties. Thus the 11th Brigade became mainly German, the 12th mainly Italian, the 13th mainly Slav and Balkan, the 14th mainly French and Belgian, and the 15th an English-speaking brigade (though originally this most cosmopolitan of all the brigades included men from a total of 26 countries). After August 1937 a complete Spanish battalion was added to each brigade (e.g. the 59th Bn. to the 15th Int. Bde.); the brigades were incorporated more closely into the Popular Army and given the status of 'shock units' (*battalons de choque*).

Many of the members of the Lincoln Battalion were students or seamen. Those of the MacKenzie-Papineau Bn. (the MacPaps or 'Fighting Canucks') from Canada and the USA were drawn from the unemployed: in September

British ambulance drivers in Barcelona 1937. Many medical units remained separate from the International Brigades, though some were incorporated into the Brigades' medical services, and many drivers and stretcher-bearers were killed at the front. Note here the popular and ubiquitous leather jacket with breeches and laced field boots. The two Spanish infantrymen wear khaki mono overalls with standard Spanish leather M1926 equipment and M1916 'short' Spanish Mauser rifles. (IBMA)

Ambulance drivers at Casa del Campo, Madrid, 1936. They wear mainly Spanish helmets and what appear to be standard Spanish issue khaki uniforms; three have medical service insignia on their lapels. (IBMA) Note Czech helmets at left, and Maltese cross painted on Spanish M1926 helmets at right – see Plate H3.

1936, for example, 1,000 unemployed in Winnipeg asked the Canadian Prime Minister to provide for their transport to Spain. The British Bn. consisted of workers and unemployed as well as the more politically active. The Irish units of the Lincoln (James Connolly Section) and British Bns. included men who had fought against the British in the Irish Republican Army. They, like the Italians, found themselves up against fellow countrymen, since other Irishmen fought with the Nationalists as part of 'General' Eaion O'Duffy's 'Blueshirts' – an ineffective unit that was not to survive long. Cuban exiles from the Batista dictatorship found their way into the Cuban Section of the Lincoln Battalion.

(In this text, and the accompanying tables, the military personnel sent to Spain by the USSR are omitted, since they operated separately from the International Brigades. Their numbers are the subject of much debate and estimates vary between several hundred and several thousand. They, like their opponents of the Condor Legion, mainly served as technical advisers and cadre in, for example, the tank and artillery arms, and as air force pilots.)

ORGANISATION

The following notes are based on the organisation recorded by Andreu Castells; but they represent an ideal seldom achieved in practice. The International Brigades were in action continuously on almost every front, and their heavy losses forced many improvisations to be made in the field.

Headquarters

International Brigade Headquarters was initially at Albacete and later at Barcelona. It comprised the Jefatura or Staff, headed by Commandant Andre Marty, with an HQ protection company; the political commissariat, headed by Luigi Longo ('Gallo'); and sections dealing with personnel, instruction and archives; operations, observation and cartography; information, censorship and discipline; commissariat, munitions, transport and administration.

The *Medical Services* were very well organised, and included many foreign volunteers; their experience was later utilised in some armies of World War II.

The *technical services and supporting arms* were

very largely Spanish. There were a few armoured cars and lorries; cavalry support was apparently entirely Spanish, and the same was true of the weak anti-aircraft defence, engineer and fortification companies and battalions. Apart from a few small units such as brigade anti-tank batteries, for example the John Brown Artillery Battery, all artillery support was Spanish.

Brigade organisation

Each Brigade in the Ejercito Popular Republicano was organised, in theory, on the pattern of the Soviet Red Army 'mixed brigade' (Brigada Mixta). The nucleus was four infantry battalions supported by a number of brigade services, as in the following list for the 15th International Brigade. However, the exigencies of continual front-line deployment as Shock Battalions and as part of the Army of Manoeuvre forced constant improvisation, and not all of this structure was in place all, or even most, of the time.

15th International Brigade

HQ: Commandant; advisor (usually a Red Army officer); adjutant; chief of staff, and secretary; chief of services; commissar of services; instructor; interpreters; public relations personnel; chief commissar, vice-commissars, commissars and adjutants; editor of brigade magazine; chronicler; chief of documents and maps section, and adjutant; chief of operations, and adjutant; sections for topography, information, commissariat, munitions, transport and brigade motor park, paymaster, medical, and communications services; catering, post office, runners. Anti-tank battery (mainly British); cavalry squadron (briefly, if at all).

Most of these positions and sections are self-explanatory, but it should be noted that Political Commissars were also included at brigade, battalion and company level, on the model of the Red Army. Mostly Communist Party members, their role was to inspire high discipline and loyalty; they had an educational and propaganda function, and were also consulted by line commanders about most decisions. In their 'psychological warfare' role they sometimes used loudspeaker vans to broadcast to the Nationalist lines – an activity that made them unpopular with the troops, since it tended to attract enemy fire.

Infantry Battalions
(not all simultaneously – see Table C)

EP 57th Bn. 'Battalon Ingles' (British, etc.)
EP 58th Bn. 'Abraham Lincoln'
(US, Canadian, etc.)
EP 59th Bn. 'George Washington'
(US, Canadian, etc.)
EP 60th Bn. 'MacKenzie-Papineau'
(US, Canadian, etc.)
EP 55th Bn. '6th February' (Franco-Belgian)
EP 59th Bn. 'Dimitrov'
(12 nationalities, mainly Balkan)
EP 59th Bn. (Spanish)
EP 48th or 49th (?) Bn. 'Tchapiaev'
(Balkan) (briefly)
Spanish Bn. 'Galindo' (briefly)

Theoretical battalion organisation

The British Battalion was ideally organised as follows, casualties and resources allowing:

Battalion commander (usually a captain) and adjutant, battalion commissar and adjutant, interpreter, chronicler, quartermaster/arms, medical officer, runners. (Commander and commissar of the brigade anti-tank battery were often attached.)
No. 1 Company 'Major Atlee'
No. 2 Company (machine gun co.)
No. 3 Company
No. 4 Company

Three rifle companies and one MG company was the basic structure of each battalion. Each company in the British Battalion had approximately 100 men; No. 1 Co. had 145 at one point. Led usually by a lieutenant and a commissar, each company comprised three sections, usually led by a sergeant; each section comprised three platoons of eight-plus men, usually led by a corporal.

The British Battalion's highest recorded strength was 650 men, but at that point most were Spanish; most battalions were usually under-strength through losses in action and difficulties of recruitment. International Brigade units suffered heavily through commitment as 'Shock Battalions' (in which role the British Battalion became famous

International Brigade, possibly the 11th, at Albacete base, in late 1936, showing preparations for the march into Madrid.

The men wear an assortment of headgear including black berets, leather coats, and blanket rolls. (IBMA)

in the Ejercito Popular) against heavily defended enemy positions. Eventually losses were filled by Spanish replacements; towards the end the International Brigades were mainly Spanish, and more closely integrated into the Ejercito Popular.

The British Battalion, formed at Madrigueras on 4 January 1937, was almost unique in being identified simply by its nationality rather than by the name of a hero of the left. Unsuccessful attempts were made to name the Battalion after leading Indian Communist MP, Shapurji Saklatvala.

UNIFORMS & EQUIPMENT

Throughout the war the uniforms and personal equipment issued to, or acquired by, the Internationals and the Ejercito Popular were extremely mixed. No hard and fast rules can be laid down, and the following notes are inevitably in general terms. Troops might be seen wearing mixtures of old Peninsular Army issue, foreign-made uniforms, captured material, and a wide range of civilian clothing.

Peninsular Army uniform items were of green- or brown-khaki drab of varying shades. The standard uniform had a single-breasted thigh-length *guerra* tunic with a deep fall collar, shoulder straps, four pleated patch pockets with single-button flaps, and buttoned wrist tabs. Although the Ejercito Popular seldom appeared in formal uniform, branch-of-service badges were supposed to be worn on the collar points; enlisted rank insignia were worn on the forearms. Officers' tunics were worn both open at the neck (M1922) over a khaki shirt and tie, or closed (M1926); they had shoulder straps, pointed false cuffs, pleated patch breast pockets with single-button flaps, and large set-back skirt pockets with single-button flaps; buttons were woven brown leather. Insignia of rank (see Plates I & J) were worn on the forearms, and of branch on the collar points. The large, flat-crowned khaki drab officers' peaked cap

bore insignia on the crown and band front, above a brown leather chinstrap, and for field and general ranks had gold peak braid of different widths.

The most ubiquitous civilian clothing included trousers or complete outfits made of brown corduroy; short 'windcheater' jackets (the *cazadora*) made in black or brown leather, or khaki drab cloth, with every possible variation of detail; wool sweaters; the very common *mono*, a lightweight one-piece overall, again varying enormously in detail and made in dark blue, dark brown, grey, khaki, etc. In winter a wide range of military and civilian greatcoats were worn, as was the Peninsular Army *capotemanta*, a heavy rectangular cloth poncho with a head opening, a deep button-up collar and sometimes a hood; and a variety of leather or sheepskin jerkins and coats.

Common headgear were berets, usually in khaki, brown or black; the Peninsular Army *'sabelino'* forage cap, often with its branch-colour tassel removed; in summer, the old Army floppy-brimmed khaki cotton sunhat; in winter, the *pasamontana*, a woollen balaclava helmet with a peak over the face opening (this also gave rise to a field cap made in serge material) which sometimes bore

insignia when made into a 'cap comforter' shape. Where worn, steel helmets were usually of French Adrian pattern, though numbers of the heavier Peninsular Army type – bearing a rough similarity to the German pattern, but of more rounded and outswept outline – were also issued, as were Czechoslovak, Portuguese, Italian and Soviet types in smaller numbers.

Trousers were cut straight, as semi-breeches, or as gaiter-trousers – *granaderos*; they were worn with ankle boots and rolled socks, with puttees, or – popular when available, especially among officers and volunteers – with calf-length laced field boots. In summer canvas shoes or *alpargatos* sandals were common.

The personal equipment of the rank and file was mainly Spanish 1926 brown leather issue. A belt with a 'clipped square' brass plate bearing branch insignia, or a frame buckle, and triple rigid leather pouches for rifle ammunition, might be supported by leather Y-straps; large cylindrical leather pouches for hand grenades were also occasionally seen. An alternative was the cavalry issue bandolier of ammunition clip pockets. (The Mills pattern webbing equipment worn in Morocco by

Staff of International Brigade, possibly the 11th, at Albacete base. Some Spanish M1926 helmets are in evidence. Several wear the black beret, and some the officer's cap of the Peninsular Army, with assorted tunics, greatcoats and storm jackets. The figure on the extreme left seems to be wearing a chest patch with three stars in a row, the rank insignia of a colonel in the Peninsular Army, thus dating this photograph to around October/November 1936 before the introduction of new insignia. (IBMA)

Spanish troops during the Rif War does not seem to have been issued widely, if at all.) A neutral-coloured canvas haversack with a leather buckled flap strap, some kind of light metal canteen in a fabric carrier, and a civilian blanket in a horseshoe roll would complete the kit of even the best-equipped Republican troops.

Uniforms

The early international volunteer units wore the most heterodox outfits, made up of whatever military or suitable civilian clothing was available. The Tom Mann Centuria wore mainly long-cut shorts and civilian shirts. Other units, e.g. the Gaston Sozzi Centuria, achieved a more military look, some officers even wearing Peninsular Army caps and ranking. At this date the *mono* or brown corduroy clothing were almost synonymous with Republican troops.

The 11th and 12th Int. Bdes. at Madrid seem to have worn much corduroy, with Spanish Army issue M1926 or Adrian steel helmets. Photos and eyewitness accounts give evidence of British leather trench jerkins or identical copies, and long leather coats, sometimes even with full military accoutrements, packs and gasmasks. The Garibaldis are supposed to have gone to the front wearing fifty per cent civilian clothing and a wide variety of weapons and equipment. It is stated that early North American volunteers for the Abraham Lincoln Bn. acquired US Army surplus M1901 series web equipment, sheepskin jackets, 'brogan' shoes and dark blue shirts before leaving the USA. The equipment was supposedly abandoned at Albacete but taken up by other units – photos of the Lincolns at the front show only individual examples of M1910 webbing.

It is stated that soon after Albacete was established as the Brigades' base area in October 1936, the quartermaster branch acquired large quantities of French Army surplus uniforms, presumably either of M1915 or M1920/35 patterns. This presents a problem for the researcher, since study of dozens of photos of troops at the front fails to reveal a single example of a French tunic – its lack of breast pockets being an unmistakable identifying feature. Certainly large numbers of Adrian helmets were supplied, of both M1916 and M1926 patterns (without, apparently, frontal badges; red stars were sometimes painted on in Republican use). French greatcoats could well feature in many photos, though in French service these lacked epaulettes, and many photos show this feature in Spanish use. The khaki woollen half-breeches or *pantalons-culottes* of French pattern may also feature in Spanish Civil War photos. Certainly, brown-khaki berets of various sizes appear in many pictures, some unmistakably of the very large French pattern.

The photographic record shows enormous variation within units; but if there was anything approaching a standard item in the Int. Bdes. it was a hip-length blouse or *cazadora* of various shades of khaki drab. Many seem clearly to have been cut down from the pre-war *guerra* four-pocket tunic; others seem to have been made 'from scratch' and lack the latter's identifying features such as the buttoning cuff-tabs and epaulettes. Photos of groups from the 15th Int.Bde. show these blouses far outnumbering but not entirely replacing the full-length tunic. They were worn – often within the same section – with a mixture of half-breeches and puttees, and very full-cut straight trousers (some with forward-buttoning pocket flaps) gathered at the ankle. A unit might wear a mixture of black, khaki, and brown berets, *isabellinos*, and *pasamontanas*; the latter were probably the most common headgear throughout the

15th Int. Bde. and many other units. Equally, group photos show a predominance of Adrian helmets, but often mixed with Czech M1930 and Spanish types.

By the time of Jarama and Brunete the 'uniform' described above was probably the most common among the Internationals, with standard Spanish M1926 leather equipment. Although much material was lost in these battles, the same outfits were still in use as late as Teruel the following January, and the MacKenzie-Papineau Bn. were issued them at Albacete in time for their baptism of fire at Fuentes de Ebro. In autumn 1937 the Internationals' closer integration into the Ejercito Popular was supposed to bring fuller Republican uniform issue, including the special Internationals' distinction of the three-pointed red star badge; but the latter was very rarely seen on uniform, and the degree to which the former was achieved is questionable. Alvah Bessie, who enlisted in the Lincolns in January 1938, recalled that quartermasters:

'. . . Handed us a neatly tied-up bundle of clothes. This bundle contained a heavy undershirt and drawers, a pair of socks, a knitted sleeveless sweater, a pair of pants (breeches, or long baggy

Italians, possibly of the Garibaldi Bn., 12th Int. Bde., El Escorial near Madrid, with the Guadarrama mountains as a backdrop. The figure on the left wears a capote-manta. *That on the right, a red star badge on a* pasamontaña. *The cold weather gear would indicate December 1936/January 1937, perhaps at the time of the battle of the Corunna road; the 12th Int. Bde. were in the vicinity of El Escorial. (IBMA)*

The Thaelmann Grupo of German anti-fascist Militias, possibly late summer 1936.

little uniformity. The Spanish Army's *granadero* gaiter-trousers were used to some extent; and canvas shoes, *alpargato* espadrilles and sandals were all common. In winter men wrapped themselves in anything they could get; at Teruel the Lincolns even plundered costumiers, taking flashy civilian suits, loud shirts and sombreros. Constantly in action, and seldom turned out for parades, the Brigaders had little interest in military splendour as long as they had the wherewithal to fight.

Some officers and NCO's, though by no means all, acquired Ejercito Popular peaked caps with the Republic's red star and appropriate badges of rank – even, occasionally, the full service dress uniform of Spanish M1922 pattern with Republican insignia added, wearing them with Sam Browne belts and sidearms (see Plate B3). For most officers, however, the normal field uniform was a black or brown beret with a rank patch; a leather jacket of 'windcheater' style; trousers or breeches; and laced field boots. Rank patches were supposed to be worn on the left chest of the field uniform, but many officers never acquired insignia, being known to their men.

Weapons

Acquisition of weapons was always a problem for the Republic. The French Popular Front government initially made some available, but closed its frontiers on 8 August 1936; thereafter the Western powers followed a 'neutral' policy of 'non-intervention', which in practice denied the Republic vital supplies, while the fascist powers continued to supply the Nationalists unhampered. Only the USSR and Mexico sold weapons to the Republic on anything like a regular basis. (The first Soviet shipments of T-26 tanks, armoured cars, artillery, motor transport and aircraft arrived by late October 1936.) The Ejercito Popular therefore took to the field with a very mixed array of small arms and support weapons of different calibres and often of obsolete patterns and poor quality, giving brigade quartermasters and armourers endless problems.

Soviet weapons known to have been used by the International Brigades included: 7.62mm M1891/30 Mosin-Nagant rifles, Degtyarev PPD

trousers that tied at the ankle), a heavy tunic, a woolly cap that could be pulled down around the ears, an overcoat or a woollen poncho. The caps, coats, jackets, overcoats and ponchos were grey, green, olive-drab, khaki, of all manner of styles; no two looked alike. They were apparently the hand-me-downs of a dozen different foreign armies (there were even clothes with the United States Army's eagle-stamped buttons).... (*Men in Battle*)

In summer there was apparently some issue of lighter khaki drill clothing, supposedly of a greenish shade; but photos of such clothing in use show

and DP M1928 light machine guns, Maxim PM1910 heavy machine guns, and 37mm M1930 L/45 anti-tank guns.

Contemporary accounts from the brigades mention many other rifle types, including particularly: Spanish 7mm M1893 and M1913 and 7.65mm Mausers (the standard Peninsular Army small arms series); Canadian .303in. Ross Mk 3B (accurate, but so dangerously unreliable that it was withdrawn from the Canadian Army after 1915); Austrian 7.9mm M1913 Steyrs (Mauser-type weapons made for Afghanistan, captured by the British from the Turkish Army in the First World War); so-called 'Mexicanskis' (Mosin-Nagants made by Remington in the USA for the Tsarist army, 1914–17; sold to Mexico by the USSR, and subsequently offered to Spain); French 8mm Lebels; US 30.06 Springfields and P17s; Swiss Veterlis; and Japanese M1907 6.5mm Arisakas. Machine guns included the excellent US .30 Lewis and .30 M1895 Colt-Browning, the old but reliable French strip-fed 8mm Hotchkiss, and the French M1915 'Chauchat' (probably the worst light machine gun ever devised). Grenades included Mills and Lafitte ('Castillo') types. Pistols of a huge variety were carried by officers, including Spanish Astras, Llamas and Stars, and German Mausers and Lugers.

The British Bn. fought at Jarama with the Steyr rifle; it was apparently reliable, but had to be loaded round by round since no charger clips were available. Later they received 'Mexicanskis', as used by the Lincolns at Jarama.

BRIGADES IN ACTION

The Spanish War had been raging for almost four months before the first of the International Brigades made their first appearance in action in Madrid on 8 November 1936.

The militias, together with loyal sections of the pre-war army, police and paramilitary services and others had denied the Nationalists the quick victory they hoped for and had successfully defended Madrid, Barcelona, Valencia, Alicante and Bilbao. Almost two-thirds of mainland Spain remained in Republican hands – a remarkable feat when one considers that most of the senior officers had gone over to the Nationalists, and that the Nationalist army was far better trained and more professional at this stage than almost anything the Republic had.

In the battle of the Sierras (22 July–August 1936) north of Madrid, the Republican militias and other units stopped General Mola's troops making further encroachments on that front. The front line generally followed the highest ridges of the natural fortress of the Sierra Guadarrama from Somosierra in the north to Alto del Leon in the south. Madrid was safe from encirclement for the time being.

In Aragon the Catalan militias, of various political hues including the early International units mentioned above, had set out on 25 July 1936, and eventually secured a front stretching from Jaca and Huesca in the north down to Belchite and Teruel. In the Basque country and Asturias the Ejercito Nacionalista Vasco, together with local militia and some involvement from early International units, secured the north for the Republic. In the parched south-western territories of Andalusia and Estremadura the Army of Africa's advance had been slowed by the local militias and others, although Cadiz, Seville (18 July 1936) and Badajoz (14 August) were taken early on; Granada (24 July) and Cordoba were also taken by the Nationalists, but these cities were cut off from the Nationalist bridgeheads further south by Republican-held territory. The Nationalists only secured Galicia, Leon, Old Castile and parts of Aragon at an early stage. Most major cities were denied to them, although they had Zaragoza, Valladolid, Burgos and Pamplona.

There now began a relentless drive by the Nationalists up the Tagus valley for Madrid. Although the militias fought bravely they were gradually rolled back north-eastwards towards the capital. General Franco then made what was probably an error and diverted his forces to relieve Col. Moscardo's besieged garrison at the Alcazar

The 11th Int. Bde. marching in column, possibly in mid-1937 during the Brunete campaign. (IBMA)

in Toledo on 27 September 1936, Madrid might have fallen had Franco continued his march.

On 30 September 1936 the government of the Second Spanish Republic created the Ejercito Popular Republicano (Popular Army). The militias, though brave, lacked discipline and knowledge of tactics, and a professionally trained army was needed to replace the old army, at least half of which had gone over to the Nationalists.

By 7/8 November 1936 the Army of Africa was threatening Madrid from the south-west; and it was during the heroic defence of the capital that the first of the International Brigades received their baptism of fire.

The battle for Madrid
(7–23 November 1936)

The Nationalists had reached the south-western outskirts of Madrid at the Casa del Campo (a park adjacent to the University of Madrid) on 6 November 1936, and had been held there by UGT and CNT trade union militia units and Enrique Lister's 5th Regiment. The Nationalists' plan of attack was discovered, and the strongest units were placed near the Casa del Campo and University where the major attack was to come. The 11th International Brigade (consisting of the Edgar André, Commune de Paris, and Dombrowski Bns.) under General Kleber joined their Spanish comrades there on 9 November – their baptism of fire. With the Commune de Paris Bn. were a group of British who comprised No. 4 Section of the Machine Gun Company (four Lewis guns) under their CO Fred Jones (and later John Cornford); these men had fought in the earlier militias. The Commune de Paris Bn. were sent to cliffs overlooking the Philosophy and Letters Building of the University, which had been occupied by the Nationalists. The 11th Int. Bde. was involved in fierce fighting in the Casa del Campo and stopped the Nationalist advance with heavy losses. The Commune de Paris Bn. was sent for a short while to Aravaca for an (unsuccessful) flanking attack on the Nationalists, and was then withdrawn to the now recaptured Philosophy and Letters Building. Barricades of books were used to block windows and shell holes against Nationalist fire from only 200 yards away. The Battalion was withdrawn to rest on 7 December 1936, having been almost a month in action. There were large gaps in the ranks which had to be filled by new recruits.

The battle of Boadilla
(13–25 December 1936)

The Nationalists then attempted to cut off Madrid from the north. The 11th and 12th Int.Bdes., with Spanish units and some Soviet tanks, beat the Nationalists out of Boadilla del Monte. When the enemy counter-attacked with tank and artillery support the Commune de Paris Bn. took the brunt; it lost over two-thirds of its number, and was forced to retire. The British machine gun section kept up fire until the last, the original dozen men being reduced to five; they were sent to join the shortly to be formed British Bn. at Albacete. The Nationalists took Boadilla and Villanueva de la Canada.

The Rakosi (51st) Bn. was originally in the 150th Bde. but was transferred to the 13th International. Their banner, depicted as Plate L3, is that which they had carried as a militia unit in Aragon early in the war. The Spanish helmet is common, though a few wear the large brown French beret. A central figure wears a khaki capote-manta. This battalion was composed of Hungarians, Czechs, Tartars from Turkestan, Ukrainians, Poles, Yugoslavs and Jews; it saw action at Huesca, Brunete, Belchite, Aragon, the Ebro and in Catalonia. (IBMA)

Another British group were with the Thaelmann Bn. of the 12th Int. Bde., also at Boadilla: No. 3 Section of No. 1 Company. The 12th went into action with Spanish units on 12 November 1936 at Cerro de Los Angeles, a hill which the Nationalists were threatening to take from the south; the brigade was later sent to Fuencarral in the Madrid suburbs. They fought for nearly a month on the fringes of University City, fighting for a Guardia Civil barracks and a cement works. A week's rest for the Thaelmann Bn. survivors (only 250 of the original 600) was followed by the 11th and 12th Int. Bdes. being sent to the Boadilla sector. The Thaelmanns suffered heavy losses; by their withdrawal on 25 December 1936, having stopped the Nationalist advance, there were only 40 survivors, including just two of the original 18 British. The actions of the International Brigades had helped prevent the encirclement of Madrid, and few advances in these sectors were made by the Nationalists for the duration of the war.

The Cordoba Front
(12 December 1936–2 January 1937)

In mid-December 1936 the Nationalist Gen. Gonzalo Queipo de Llano started an offensive from Cordoba and Granada aimed at Andujar. The militias did the best they could, but after ten days' fighting the road to Madrid was open. The 14th Int. Bde., with other Republican units of a newly created Army of the South under Gen. Martinez Monje, was sent to check the Nationalist advance. The 14th were mainly French and Belgians, commanded by Gen. Walter; its La Marseillaise Bn. was strengthened by the addition of No. 1 Co. of 145 British (with some Irish, Cypriots and Dutch) commanded by George Nathan - some of them had fought in Madrid but most had little training.

The 14th left Albacete on Christmas Day 1936 and, after enduring strafing by Nationalist aircraft, reached Lopera on 28 December 1936. No. 1 Co. led the advance to take Lopera; they were confronted by heavy fire from machine guns, artillery and aircraft, and reached the outskirts suffering heavy losses. Ralph Fox, the commissar, was killed, and so too was John Cornford trying to

A group of the British (57th) Battalion, 15th Int. Bde.: Scottish, Irish and Welsh members displaying their own unofficial pennant. Probably photographed during the long vigil in the Jarama trenches between February and June 1937, practically all have the pasamontana, well illustrated here folded into a peaked field cap. Note the short jacket or blouse, known as a cazadora, on the left. The Irish had their own section in the British Bn. first commanded by Kit Conway, killed at Jarama. Another Irish contingent, the James Connolly Section, were in the Lincoln Battalion. (IBMA)

reach him. No. 1 Co. was forced to retire, and the rest of the battalion was in even worse shape than the disciplined British. On 29 December the Nationalists attacked in force, and No. 1 Co. was again forced back after standing its ground as long as possible. The Battalion CO, Maj. Gaston Delasalle, was shot for cowardice on 2 January 1937. The La Marseillaise Bn. was renamed the Ralph Fox Bn. in honour of the fallen commissar, and George Nathan was appointed commander.

The battle of the Corunna Road (3–15 January 1937)

On 3 January 1937 the Nationalists made another attempt on Madrid by a push towards the Madrid-Corunna road, northwards from Boadilla and Villanueva de la Canada. Led by tanks of the Condor Legion, five Nationalist divisions under Gen. Orgaz broke the Republican lines and eventually took Las Rozas and Majadahonda, cutting the road in several places. Facing them was Gen. Miaja's corps of five divisions, including some Soviet tanks under Gen. Pavlov, and, under Gen. Emilio Kleber, the 11th Int. Bde. (Dombrowski, Thaelmann and Edgar André Battalions). The Thaelmann and Edgar André Bns. were sent to

Las Rozas on 4 January, and the Commune de Paris Bn. to Pozuelo.

On 5 January the Republican front broke and the Nationalists pushed northwards, reaching Las Rozas and Pozuelo at the expense of heavy casualties from the machine gun units of the Internationals. On the 6th the Thaelmann Bn. was ordered to hold ground at Las Rozas, and were eventually surrounded; they held out against tanks, Moorish infantry and aircraft, but when ordered to advance on the 7th their numbers had been so depleted that they were unable to do so. They were joined on 10 January by the 14th Int. Bde. straight from the now quiet Cordoba front, and also by the 12th Int. Bde. and Lister's Brigade. They attempted to drive the Nationalists from the Las Rozas-Majadahonda road, and made advances with tank support, but bad weather and enemy tank attacks caused a standstill.

On 15 January deep snow made fighting impossible. A stalemate developed, and the 14th Int. Bde. was withdrawn to Albacete; only 67 of the original 145 men in the British No. 1 Co. remained (the company was by the end of the month incorporated into the new British Bn. of the 15th Brigade). The battle of the Corunna road

A group of the Dimitrov (59th) Bn., 15th Int. Bde. at Jarama. All wear French Adrian helmets; note Spanish belt equipment at left, and US M1910 rifle belt at right. Two have stick grenades. This crack battalion eventually went to the 129th Bde., after Belchite, and were replaced by the MacKenzie-Papineau Battalion. The Dimitrovs came from Rumania, Bulgaria, Serbia, Croatia and Albania, with some Czechs, Poles, Germans, Austrians and Italians. (BFB)

had at least prevented the Nationalists from linking up with other enemy units on the Sierra Guadarrama to the north-west: Madrid was saved from encirclement again.

The battle of Jarama
(6–27 February, and June 1937)

Having failed to take Madrid from the north and west the Nationalists tried another offensive on a ten-mile front to the south-east of the city in the Jarama valley, with the aim of cutting off the capital from its vital supply line along the Valencia road. They attacked in five brigades under Gen. Varela, each stiffened by units of Moroccans and Foreign Legionaries from the Army of Africa, supported by Condor Legion artillery. On 6 February 1937 the Nationalist commander Garcia Escamez took the railhead of Ciempozuelas at the southern end of the front, and advanced towards San Martin de la Vega and the Jarama River. Meanwhile, Rada's brigade to the north had taken the heights of La Marinosa, all but destroying two Republican battalions. Barron's brigade reached the junction of the Jarama and Manzanares Rivers on 7 February, near enough to bring the Valencia road within range. On 8 February, to stem the retreat of Republican forces, Gen. Miaja sent Lister's 11th Division under the command of Juan Modesto to join Gen. Pozas' Army of the Centre under Col. Burillo.

On 9 February a line was organised along the high ground east of the Jarama River; but on the night of the 11th a *tabor* of Moroccans under Maj. Molero took the Pindoque railway bridge in the middle of the ten-mile front by a *coup de main* against the André Marty Bn., 14th Int. Bde.; Barron's brigade were able to cross the river, but the Garibaldi Bn., 12th Int. Bde., brought the bridgehead under fire from the heights and held up Barron's further advance.

At San Martin de la Vega another Nationalist brigade had stormed the village, Moroccans taking the bridge over the Jarama by another night attack; by 12 February they were storming the heights to the west of Pingarron, and were joined by Saenz de Buruaga's brigade. Facing them was the newly formed 15th Int. Bde., consisting of the British Bn. commanded by Capt. Tom Wintringham and including the veterans of No. 1 Co.; the 6th February Bn. (Franco-Belge) and the Dimitrov Bn. (Balkans).

The 15th Int. Bde. moved up to the front from

Chinchon on 12 February. Their start point was the junction of the Madrid-Chinchon/San Martin de la Vega-Morata de Tajuna roads. Orders were given for the brigade to move towards San Martin de la Vega; the 6th February Bn. advanced along the road with the British to the left of them and the Dimitrovs in reserve. No one was to the left of the British, and their flank was open – a fact unknown at the time both to them and to the Nationalists. After a two-mile advance they came under heavy fire and withdrew to the crest of a hill (later dubbed 'Suicide Hill'), where they formed a line and engaged the Nationalists. The 6th February Bn. had also come under fire on the road and had withdrawn, leaving a knoll by the road unoccupied. The Moors quickly occupied it, and were able to direct enfilading fire onto the British Bn., which was fighting tenaciously.

Further back, across a valley between Suicide Hill and a 680-metre spur, No. 2 (MG) Co. under Lt. Harry Fry set up its eight heavy Maxims, only to find the belts filled with the wrong ammunition. They were withdrawn to the rear while the belts were loaded with the correct ammunition by hand, the machine gun company in the meantime acting as a rifle company. The veteran No. 1 Co. was on a 660-metre hill between Suicide Hill and the knoll by the road, while Nos. 3 and 4 Co. were on Suicide Hill. Heavy fire was coming at them from the front, from the knoll on their right, and from their right rear where the 6th February Bn. had withdrawn. The British Bn. took heavy casualties as a result, and were ordered to withdraw to the spur and join No. 2 Co. The Nationalists occupied Suicide Hill and the adjoining hill, and rashly moved down into the valley to take the spur; by now No. 2 Co. had its Maxims back in action, and their fire routed the advancing enemy.

By now the British had been fighting for seven hours at heavy cost, but had held the Nationalists back. A short withdrawal was made to a sunken road to reorganise the 125 men remaining out of the original 400 in the three rifle companies; less than half the battalion survived unwounded. On the spur No. 2 Co. was kept in position with No. 4 Co. to its right and No. 1 Co. to its left. In the early hours of 13 February a Nationalist unit moved into the valley but were soon forced back by No. 2 Co.'s Maxims; but the battalion was now

A group of the '6th February' Bn., 15th Int. Bde. in the Jarama trenches, spring 1937. The Adrian helmet and black or brown berets are worn with a variety of uniforms. This Franco-Belgian battalion was down to less than one company at Brunete, and was eventually incorporated into the 14th ('La Marseillaise') Int. Bde. composed mainly of their fellow countrymen. (BFB)

Trenches of the Abraham Lincoln Bn. at Jarama. The photograph was obviously taken after the worst of the fighting, as the trenches are dug deep. (BFB)

in a serious position, as the 6th February Bn. and the Dimitrovs had been pushed even further back and the British Bn. was surrounded on three sides. No. 4 Co. was withdrawn without orders, leaving No. 2 Co. unsupported. Soon afterwards a party of Nationalists infiltrated their position due to some kind of mistake over their identity – a mistake which resulted in the Nationalists shooting three men and taking 30 prisoners. The remains of No. 4 Co. (40 men) charged the captured position to no avail, and only six returned.

On the night of 13 February the 160 survivors of the battalion formed a defensive line along the sunken road. On the 14th a fresh Nationalist brigade attacked, supported by tanks. With no anti-tank guns, the British broke and fell back to the Chinchon road. Jock Cunningham and Frank Ryan rallied the 140 tired survivors, and they marched back up the San Martin road singing, joined on the way by other Republican groups. The enemy fell back from the spur to their earlier positions; and later that day fresh Republican units were brought up. The line had held, owing to the efforts of the British Bn. in its first action; and the Nationalists advanced no further on this front for the remainder of the war.

To the north of the 15th Int. Bde. the 11th, 14th and 12th Int. Bdes. were also in the line along with Spanish units, and eventually held a front-line just east of the Chinchon-Madrid road towards the Arganda bridge. On 16 February the newly formed Abraham Lincoln Bn. of the 15th Int. Bde. reached the front, receiving its baptism of fire on the 23rd. Lister's Bde. moved up to the left of the 15th, which was strengthened by the addition of the North Americans, a Spanish battalion and 85 newly arrived British. The subsequent actions on the Jarama front consisted of typical trench warfare, with both sides trying to improve their positions. On 27 February the 15th Int. Bde. was ordered forward without air and artillery support. Heavy machine gun fire brought the British advance to a halt within a few yards, though the Lincolns gained several hundred yards, at the cost of 127 dead and 200 wounded, before being forced to retire under cover of darkness.

The 15th Int. Bde. remained in the Jarama trenches for five months, being joined in early June by its newly formed anti-tank battery (largely British) with its three Soviet 37mm guns; these were immediately put to use in knocking out Nationalist machine gun positions.

The result of Jarama was that the Nationalists advanced to a depth of at most ten miles on a front ten–fifteen miles long; but they were denied their objective, the Madrid-Valencia road, which remained a vital supply route for the Republic. All this cost some 10,000 Republican casualties and 6,000 on the Nationalist side.

The battle of Guadalajara (8–18 March 1937)

Having failed in their attempts to enter Madrid from the north and the south-west, and to cut off the capital from the Valencia road at Jarama, the Nationalists made what was to be their final attempt to encircle Madrid from the north-east, around Guadalajara; the battle is really misnamed, since all the action took place around the pueblos of Trijueque and Brihuega, some 20 miles from the town. The Nationalist attempt on Guadalajara was part of a wider plan to link up with the Nationalist armies near the Jarama and thus to encircle Madrid. The Nationalists were organised in five divisions: the Soria Division under Moscardo (15,000 Moors and some Carlists); three Italian Fascist 'Blackshirt' Divisions (35,000) under the overall command of Gen. Roatta – the 'Dio lo Vuole' Division (Rossi), Black Flames Division (Coppi), and Black Arrows Division (Nuvoloni); and one Italian regular army formation, the 'Littorio' Division (Bergonzoli). This force enjoyed considerable motor transport, armour and artillery support as well as air cover.

The Black Flames Division pushed back the Republican 12th Division under Col. Lacalle, and the Soria Division broke through on the Soria road but Roatta's Italians encountered stiff resistance at Brihuega on 10 March from the Republican 4th Army Corps of three divisions under Jurado. The 11th Division (under Enrique Lister) consisted of the 11th Int. Bde. (re-formed Thaelmann, Edgar André and Commune de Paris Bns.), El Campesino's Bde. and two other Spanish brigades. The 14th Division (under Cipriano Mera) included the 12th Int. Bde. (Garibaldi, Dombrowski and André Marty Bns.), and the Spanish 65th brigade. Col. Lacalle's 12th Division comprised the 49th, 50th and 61st brigades. Some Soviet tanks and aircraft were also available. The 11th Int. Bde. was now more than 50 per cent Spanish owing to the appalling losses in the battles around Madrid, and there were upwards of 35-45 per cent Spanish in the 12th.

These divisions established a front spanning the Madrid-Guadalajara road, with the 11th Division between Trijueque and Torija, the 14th Division along the Brihuega-Torija road, and the 12th Division in reserve. Near Brihuega, which the Italians took on 10 March, stood the Ibarra Palace. The 12th Int. Bde. advanced from Torija towards Brihuega, unaware that it had been taken; they encountered some Italian patrols. The 11th Int. Bde. made contact with the 12th, and very soon some tanks attached to the Black Flames Division appeared and were fired on by machine gunners of the Garibaldi battalion. Some units of the Black Flames infantry were sent forward, and asked their fellow Italians why they had been fired on; when they discovered that the Garibaldis were Republicans they surrendered, but for most of 10 and 11 March the Garibaldis and the Black Flames Division fought a 'civil war within a civil

Men of the British Bn. on 48 hours' leave in Madrid during the Jarama campaign of spring 1937. All four wear a buttoned-flap cap which seems to have originated with the pasamontana, but apart from that they display an assortment of ill-fitting gear. See Plate D2. (IBMA)

A meeting of No. 1 Co. of the British Bn., the Jarama area, May 1937. Note the variety of headgear and clothing and Moisin-Nagant rifles with long bayonets stacked against the bank. IBMA/BA)

war' around the Ibarra Palace.

Meanwhile, the Black Arrows had broken through Republican 11th Division to take Trijueque and began a furious drive towards Torija. The 11th Int. Bde. suffered heavy casualties, but held the road from Torija to Trijueque. The road to Trijueque from Brihuega was also held on 11 March by the Garibaldi Battalion. Amazingly, Gen. Roatta ordered a day of rest on 12 March for the Italian divisions; this permitted the Republican air force to bomb and strafe the stationary units.

The Republican 11th Division then counter-attacked with armoured support. The Thaelmann and El Campesino Bdes. recaptured Trijueque at bayonet point, and many Italians surrendered; the Garibaldis continued their assault towards Brihuega, and captured the Ibarra Palace as night fell on 12 March. On 13 March Roatta called up his reserve divisions; these attacks were beaten off by the Republicans, and on 14 March Pavlov's tanks drove beyond Trijueque towards Siguenza and captured much Nationalist material.

After a three-day lull the Republicans went onto the offensive on 18 March supported by over 100 aircraft and a heavy artillery barrage. The 11th and 14th Divisions, with 70 Soviet tanks, pushed forward and the Italians were rapidly routed. The Republicans regained some ground, although the Nationalists retained some territory (about 12 miles deep) which they did not hold on 8 March. Overall it represented a defeat for the Nationalists, as their aim of encircling Madrid was frustrated. The Italian dictator Mussolini, in a fit of rage, ordered that no Italian expeditionary troops were to be given home leave in Italy until this disgrace had been retrieved by an Italian victory. The battle was also a huge propaganda victory for the Republic, as it proved to the world that Franco was relying on foreign intervention in his supposed war of national unity.

This battle ended the Nationalist attempts to encircle Madrid, and the battle fronts thus established remained until 1 April 1939. The laurels of victory at Guadalajara have gone to the Garibaldi Bn., though it should be remembered that far larger numbers of Spaniards fought there. Franco next concentrated on the north, which finally fell

Two men of the Garibaldi Bn., 12th Int. Bde. during the battle of Guadalajara, where this battalion fought and defeated Italian Fascist units. They wear Spanish tabardo jackets, the figure on the right with a Spanish M1926 helmet. See plate F2. (IBMA)

on 19 June 1937 after his capture of Bilbao. No International Brigades were employed on this northern front.

The battle of Brunete
(6–26 July 1937)

Having fended off several Nationalist assaults against Madrid, the Republican command under Gen. José Miaja felt confident enough to launch their first offensive at Brunete to the west of the capital. The goal was to force a salient into enemy lines and to place pressure on the Nationalist troops at the Casa del Campo, so that they would withdraw from that front, and also to help relieve pressure on the hard-pressed northern front in Asturias.

The Republican forces consisted of two army corps comprising 80–90,000 personnel. The 5th Corps under Juan Modesto comprised the 11th Division (Lister), 46th Division (El Campesino) and the 35th Division (Walter), the latter including the 11th International Brigade. The 18th Corps under Jurado comprised the 15th Division (Gal), including the 13th and 15th Int. Bdes., the 34th Division (Galan), and the 10th Division (Enciso), plus three artillery groups and an armoured battalion. The 15th Int. Bde. (Lt. Col. Copic) included the British Bn., the Lincoln Bn., the Washington Bn., the 6th February Bn., the Dimitrov Bn., and the newly formed anti-tank

battery. The 2nd Corps (five brigades plus artillery and armoured cars) was to assemble south of Madrid. There was also a reserve force of two divisions (five brigades); one of these was the 45th (Kleber) including the 12th International Brigade. Also present were the 13th, 68th and 71st Divisions. In all there were 23 Spanish brigades, five of Internationals (including the 14th, who were not directly involved), as well as Soviet advisors, 130 tanks, 40 armoured cars and 188 field guns, plus 200 aircraft.

On the night of 6 July the 5th and 18th Corps moved silently into the foothills of the Guadarrama Mountains south of the El Escorial-Madrid road on a ten-kilometre front stretching from the Perales River in the west to the Aulencia River in the east. The aim was to push southward to Brunete and then eastward to Boadilla del Monte, and also southwards to outflank the Nationalists besieging Madrid. In this salient there were no more than 2,000 Nationalist troops; but stronger enemy forces were nearby, including the 7th Corps (Varela) comprising the 71st and 72nd Divisions (51,400 men), and the 1st Corps (54,300 men) comprising the 11th Division (Irutetago-yena), 12th Division (Asensio) and 14th Division (Juan Yagüé). Together with another corps on the Aragon front this force constituted the Nationalist Army of the Centre under Gen. Saliquet. One division (the 13th) was held in reserve nearby under Barron.

The Nationalists were largely taken by surprise; although they knew that an attack was likely near Quijorna they underestimated its scale, believing the main offensive would come on the River Ebro in Aragon. There was also a feint attack on the Jarama. Only two *tabors* of Moroccans (700 men) were sent to the Brunete area, and initially only 2,700 Nationalists faced the Republican onslaught. On 6 July Modesto's 5th Corps advanced on their sector between Quijorna and Villanueva de la Canada. The 46th and 35th Divisions speedily took the Quijorna sector, and Lister's 11th Division swept on to Brunete and surrounded it after a spectacular ten-mile advance. 18th Corps (Jurado) aimed for Villanueva de la Canada and beyond it to the Brunete-Boadilla road. The brunt of the fighting in the Villanueva de la Canada sector fell to the 13th and 15th Int. Bdes.; a Spanish unit supported by tanks had failed to take the heavily defended town of Villanueva, and the 15th Int. Bde. were ordered into the 'furnace of Brunete'. The 15th Bde. surrounded the town, with the British Bn. to the south straddling the Brunete road, but pinned down by enemy machine gunners in the church tower. Towards dusk the Nationalists launched a sortie behind a human shield of civilians; it was beaten off, at a tragic cost. In failing light the British, Lincoln and Dimitrov Bns. and a Spanish brigade assaulted the village and wiped out the last resisting Nationalists. Fifty members of the British Bn. had been lost.

Next morning the 15th Int. Bde. swept eastwards towards the heights beyond the Guadarrama River commanding the villages of Romanillos and Boadilla del Monte, and made preparations to assault Mosquito Ridge the next day; but by the 8th Mosquito Ridge was held by a considerable force of Nationalist troops well dug in. Over the next two days repeated attempts were made to take it, but enemy firepower from the heights, unbearable heat, and Nationalist command of the air took their toll among the attackers. By 11 July the Nationalists had recovered from their initial surprise; Franco switched Gen. Varela with 30,000 troops from the Santander front, and counter-attacked heavily.

The 15th Int. Bde., withdrawn a mile behind the front, had suffered appalling casualties. The Washington Bn., bombed in the open, had now to be merged with the Lincolns. The British Bn. had only 150 fit men out of approximately 300, but were ordered back into the line when an inexperi-

Machine gunners of No. 2 Co., British Bn., 15th Int. Bde. during the battle of Brunete, July 1937; they wear French helmets and khaki shirts, and are firing Soviet Maxim machine guns. (BFB)

Members of the Sanidad Militar *during the battle of Brunete, July 1937. An ambulance, many of which were donated to Spain, can be seen in the background, along with* *two Soviet T-26 tanks. Note 'Y' straps of soldier in the foreground; and the caps of the stretcher bearers, which seem to have been fairly popular – see Plate F1. (IBMA)*

enced Spanish unit gave ground. On 18 July Varela mounted a counter-offensive with overwhelming aircraft and artillery support. Lister's 11th Division, forced out of Brunete, fought their way back in only to be driven out a second time. Their retreat left the British Bn., reduced to 100 men, exposed on Mosquito Ridge, and a fighting withdrawal started. Back across the Guadarrama River the British Bn. were found to have only 42 able-bodied men left.

By 25 July the Nationalist counter-offensive had spent itself, and the line began to stabilise roughly from Quijorna in the west to just north of Brunete, and on to Villanueva del Castillo and near Villanueva del Pardillo in the north. The Republic had gained ground to a depth of four miles on a ten-mile front, but failed to achieve their objectives. The Internationals, some of the Republic's best troops at this time, had fought bravely but at terrible cost. The Nationalist counter-attack won back about six miles of territory. Both sides claimed Brunete as a victory; but the inexperience of the Republic's commanders had resulted in fatal confusion and a costly failure to exploit initial gains.

The Republican Aragon offensive (24 August–October 1937)

It was in the largely quiet Aragon sector that the Republic was to launch its next offensive. The Aragon front stretched from near Jaca in the north southwards to Huesca, and near Quinto and Belchite down to Teruel; inland from here it linked up with Guadalajara. It had seen little activity since the Catalan militias had come out to confront the Nationalists in the autumn of 1936. (George Orwell had served with the POUM Militia on this front, along with several future International Brigaders.)

The Republic had amassed an Army of the East with 80,000 troops, 100 tanks and 200 aircraft under the overall command of the Catalan Gen. Sebastian Pozas. Their objective was Zaragoza and the towns and villages to the east of it. The reconstituted 5th Corps comprised some of the divisions which had fought at Brunete: the 11th (Lister); 15th, including the 13th Int. Bde.; 35th (Walter), including the 11th, 14th and 15th Int. Bdes.; 45th (Kleber), including the 12th Int. Bdes.

and 46th (El Campesino). The main aim of this offensive was to relieve pressure on the northern front around Santander in the Basque country. Nationalist forces in Zaragoza were under the command of Gen. Ponte, in Huesca under Gen. Urrutia and in Teruel under Gen. Munoz Castellanos.

The Ejercito Republicano Popular attacked at eight points on 24 August 1937, with little artillery or aerial support. In the Huesca sector three attacks were made involving the 45th Division including the 12th (Garibaldi) Int. Bde.; three attacks were also made in the south near Teruel, and two between Belchite and Zaragoza, these latter involving the 35th Division with its three International Brigades. (The International Brigades now included considerable numbers of volunteer Spanish troops from other units.)

The 15th Int. Bde. under Lt. Col. Vladimir Copic now comprised the British Bn. (400 men, of whom 200 were British), the British Anti-Tank battery, the Dimitrov Bn., the Spanish 24th Bn. and the Lincoln Bn.; the MacKenzie-Papineau Bn. were to join later.

On 24 August 1937 the 15th Int. Bde. began its assault on Quinto, which straddles the Zaragoza highway south of the River Ebro. The British Bn. and the Spanish 24th were initially kept in reserve

Posed photo of members of the Abraham Lincoln Bn. taken before the battle of Brunete. Note Czech and French helmets, berets, variety of gear, and 'Mexicanski' rifles with long bayonets. The Canadian section leader Sgt. Armitage, kneeling third from right, was killed at Villanueva de la Canada. (IBMA)

and it fell to the other two battalions to take the small town, whose strongest point was a fortified church. The Lincoln Bn. bore the brunt of the fighting, while the anti-tank battery fired into the church to quell enemy machine gun fire. After fierce house-to-house fighting, with the Lincolns flushing out Nationalist snipers with grenades, something had to be done about the church, whose windows bristled with enemy machine guns. Ten Lincolns led by Carl Bradley, and armed with nitro-glycerine bottles, crept up to the church, which was being battered by the anti-tank battery, and flushed out the Nationalists.

The 15th Int. Bde. were then ordered to Belchite to help complete its capture; on the way the British were diverted to take Mediana, to prevent a Nationalist relief column going to the assistance of Belchite; meanwhile, the rest of the brigade were committed to fierce street fighting in Belchite. The anti-tank battery fired over 2,700 shells into the town in support of the Lincolns

Officer of the International Brigades, possibly of the medical services. His dress is typical of officers on active service: a khaki beret with rank insignia and a common soldier's khaki uniform. (IBMA)

these units came under murderous fire; and the attempt to take Zaragoza was finally abandoned. The 15th spent another ten days in the trenches facing the Nationalists, but bad weather brought all fighting to a standstill in October.

On 23 September 1937 a Republican decree formalised the status and organisation of the International Brigades which, although they were numbered according to the Ejercito Popular Republicano brigade sequence, had enjoyed some autonomy. The brigades were now incorporated formally into the Ejercito Popular; and most initially became part of the Army of Manoeuvre under overall command of Gen. Vicente Lluch Rojo, one of the most able Republican generals. The International Brigades by now contained large numbers of Spanish volunteers, and 'Internationals' had to undertake to remain until the end of the war. Battalion numbering was also altered, e.g. British 57th, Lincolns 58th, Spanish 59th (ex-24th), MacPaps (60th), etc. (see Table D).

The Republican Teruel Offensive
(15 December 1937–20 February 1938)

In response to the loss of the north to Franco in October, the Republicans were to attack at Teruel, where the Nationalists held a salient into Republican territory, since the Catalan militias had taken most of the rest of Aragon in the early days of the war. The front wandered down from near Huesca, through Lecinena, Fuentes de Ebro, Fuentetodos, Martin del Rio, Utrillas and down the Sierra Palomera to Teruel, and then northeastwards near Alberracin and Molina de Aragon up to Guadalajara. The Republican Army under Hernandez Sarabia was initially to consist entirely of Spanish units comprising 18th Corps, 22nd Corps and 20th Corps; later, other units including the 11th and 15th Int. Bdes. were rushed to this sector. In Teruel itself was a 6,000-strong garrison under Col. Rey d'Harcourt, which would be reinforced after several days by the corps of Gens. Varela and Aranda under the overall command of Gen. Davila.

On 15 December 1937, in bitter cold and deep snow, the Republican attack began by a thrust to encircle the town. Three days later troops of the

and Dimitrovs as they cleared each street, house by house, digging holes in interconnecting walls with their bayonets and throwing in grenades. The fighting was also heavy around the several churches which had been fortified by the enemy as machine gun positions. Eventually, the ruins of Belchite fell to the Republican forces on 5 September 1937.

The next objective for the 15th Int. Bde. was Fuentes de Ebro; here the assault began with the Spanish 24th Bn. clinging onto the sides of Soviet tanks, but most of the men were shaken off or succumbed to Nationalist fire and the other battalions were left far behind. The British Bn. were on the right nearest to the River Ebro, with the Lincoln Bn. straddling the railway to Zaragoza, and the newly formed MacKenzie-Papineau Bn. to their left between Mediana and Fuentes. All

Table D: Infantry Battalions of the International Brigades

I.B.	E.P.		Name	Main nationalities	Brigade(s)
1st	41st	(41)	Edgar André	German	11th
2nd	56th	(42)	Commune de Paris	French/Belgian	11th, 14th
3rd	48th?	(43)	Garibaldi	Italian	12th
4th	49th	(44)	Dombrowski	Polish/Hungarian	11th, 12th
5th	42nd?	(45)	Thaelmann	German	12th, 11th
6th	46th?	(46)	Andre Marty	French/Belgian	12th, 150th
7th	47th?	(47)	Louise Michel I	French/Belgian	13th, 14th
8th	49th	(48)	Tchapiaev	Balkan	13th, 129th
9th		(49)	Nine Nations	Mixed	14th
10th	50th	(50)	Henri Vuillemin	French	13th, 14th
11th		(51)	Domingo Germinal (merged with Vaillant-Couturier)	Spanish	14th
12th		(52)	La Marseillaise	French	14th
13th	53rd	(53)	Henri Barbusse	French	14th
14th	54th	(54)	Pierre Brachet	French	14th
15th		(55)	'6th February'	French/Belgians	15th, 14th
		(56)	(Commune de Paris)		
16th	57th	(57)	British	British	15th
17th	58th	(58)	Abraham Lincoln	US	15th
18th	59th	(59)	Dimitrov	Balkan	15th, 129th, 13th
19th			'12th February'	Austrian	11th
20th	59th	(59)	George Washington (after Dimitrovs left 15th Bde.)	US	15th
20th			Veinte (20th)	Mixed	86th, 13th
21st	51st		Mathias Rakosi	Hungarian	150th, 13th
22nd	60th	(60)	MacKenzie-Papineau ('MacPaps')	Canadian/US	15th
23rd	52nd		Palafox	Polish	13th
24th	59th	(59)	Spanish (after Washingtons merged with Lincolns)	Spanish	15th
25th?	50th		Adam Mickiewicz	Polish	13th
26th			Thomas Mazaryk	Czech	129th
27th			Djure Dajakovich	Balkan	129th
28th			Vaillant-Couturier	French	14th?
			Ralph Fox (in La Marseillaise)	French/English	14th
			Hans Beimler (merged with Thaelmanns)	German/Scandinavian	11th
			Asturias Heredia	Spanish	11th
			Deda Blagoiev (merged with Djakovich)		129th
			Doce Lenguas (merged with Dimitrovs)		15th, 129th, 13th
			Figlio (merged with Garibaldi's)	Italian	12th
			Galindo	Spanish?	15th
			Madrid	Spanish	11th, 12th
51st			Juan Marco	Spanish	13th
11th?			Louise Michel II (merged with Henri Vuillemin)	French	14th
52nd			Otumba	Spanish	13th
			Pacifico	Spanish	11th
			Pasionaria	Spanish	11th
			Prieto	Spanish	12th
			Primera Unidad de Avance	Spanish	14th

Key: **IB** = Int. Bde. bn. numbering; **EP** = Ejercito Popular bn. numbering.

Note: Andreu Castells and Bob Cordery both give the above numbering, but there are inconsistencies. Since the Edgar André were certainly the 41st Bn., consecutive numbering (in brackets above) of the battalions to 60 'MacKenzie-Papineau' almost produces a perfect match. The British (57th), Lincolns (58th), Dimitrovs and later Washington and Spanish (59th), and MacKenzie-Papineau (60th) numbering is correct (source: Bill Alexander) and produces a mismatch of one. Renumbering may have taken place as battalions disbanded or merged (e.g. as with the 59th). The Spanish battalions fought for a limited time with the quoted brigade, although by the Ebro offensive many Spanish units and commanders were with the International Brigades.

December the 11th and 15th Int. Bdes. were moved up to the front; the British Bn. were initially at Cuevas Labradas to the north of Teruel. On 7 January Teruel finally fell to El Campesino's brigade. On 14 January the 15th Int. Bde. were moved to the north-east to help check the massive Nationalist counter-offensive. The MacPaps were on the left near La Muela, straddling a railway line running north to Concud; the British Bn. were on Santa Barbara hill, and the 11th Int. Bde. (Thaelmanns) were on El Muleton to the right; the Lincolns were in the town and the 59th Bn. were on La Muela.

The British Bn.'s machine gun company were on high cliffs commanding the plain stretching to Concud and beyond, with the anti-tank battery. On 17 January 1938 the Nationalists advanced near Concud and their artillery caused heavy losses amongst the Thaelmanns and MacPaps. However when the Nationalists moved nearer toward the cliffs the British machine guns took a heavy toll. On the 18th the Thaelmanns were forced off El Muleton, and the Nationalists attempted to roll up the MacPaps; again the British machine guns opened up and wrought havoc. The three British rifle companies now moved down to the plain to protect the MacPaps' flank on the left, with some Spanish Marineros to the right; a defensive line was formed on a fortified hill. On the 19th the enemy bombarded these positions, but a rash infantry attack suffered heavy casualties from the well dug-in Republican forces. Though the latter were forced back somewhat they stood their ground, and the Nationalists abandoned their attempt to recapture Teruel from that direction.

The 15th Int. Bde. conducted a diversionary action at Segura de los Banos, some 40 miles to the north, at this time.

The Nationalist counter-offensive had largely encircled the ruins of Teruel by the second week of February; and Generals Yagué and Monasterio, driving from the north, inflicted some 22,000 Republican casualties. El Campesino's 46th Bde. fought their way clear of the trap, and on 20 February Teruel was retaken by the Nationalists.

Capt. Frank Ryan, leader of Irish Volunteers for the Republic. Ryan was a journalist before volunteering in December 1936, and edited 'The Book of the 15th Brigade', a valuable reference source. Ryan, with Jock Cunningham, rallied the exhausted British Bn. at Jarama and led them back to the front to close a gap. Captured by the fascists in the Aragon retreats in March 1938; he set an example to all in captivity, and was not released in the subsequent exchanges of prisoners. Taken to Germany and kept under house arrest, he was put on a U-boat to be set ashore in Ireland to liaise with the IRA. This did not take place, however, and Ryan died of natural causes in Dresden in June 1944. He is shown here in the M1922 service uniform; note infantry branch badges on the lapels, and the three - bar rank insignia of a captain beneath a red star on his cuff. (IBMA)

18th Corps held the heights of La Muela dominating Teruel from the North. By the 25th the town had been penetrated, but the defenders continued fighting house-to-house. By 29 December Franco had ordered a counter-offensive, and Davila's troops attacked from the north; they pushed back, but did not break, the Republican lines to the north-east of the town. On 31

1: Dombrowski Bn., 11th Int. Bde.; Madrid, 1936
2: Gen. Kleber, 11th Int. Bde.; Madrid, 1936
3: Volunteer, 11th or 12th Int. Bde.; Madrid, 1936

A

1: Lt., British Bn., 15th Int. Bde., 1937
2: Officer, '6th February' Bn., 15th Int. Bde., 1937
3: Capt. Tom Wintringham, British Bn., 1937

B

1 & 2: Volunteers, British Bn.; Jarama, 1937
3: Maxim crew, No. 2 Co., British Bn.; Jarama, 1937

C

1: Volunteer, Anti-Tank Bty., 15th Int. Bde., 1937
2: Volunteer, British Bn., 15th Int. Bde., 1937
3: Volunteer, Abraham Lincoln Bn., 15th Int. Bde., 1937

D

1 & 2: Volunteers, Abraham Lincoln Bn., 15th Int. Bde.; The Ebro, July 1938
3: Volunteer, Abraham Lincoln Bn., summer 1937

2

1

3

1: Dimitrov Bn., 15th Int. Bde.; Jarama, 1937
2: Garibaldi Bn., 12th Int. Bde.; Guadalajara, 1937
3: Rakosi Bn., 13th Int. Bde., 1938

1: Capt. E. C. Smith, Mackenzie-Papineau Bn., 15th Int. Bde.; Teruel, Jan. 1938
2 & 3: Volunteers, Mackenzie-Papineau Bn., 1938

G

1: Medical volunteer: Barcelona, 1937
2: Doctor, Canadian BTU; Madrid, 1937
3: Private, Sanidad Militar; Madrid, 1936

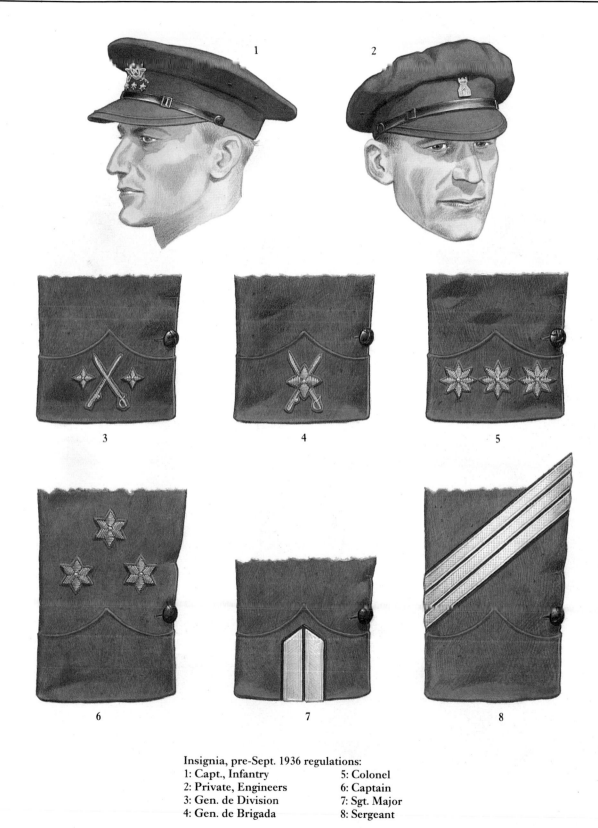

Insignia, pre-Sept. 1936 regulations:
1: Capt., Infantry   5: Colonel
2: Private, Engineers   6: Captain
3: Gen. de Division   7: Sgt. Major
4: Gen. de Brigada   8: Sergeant

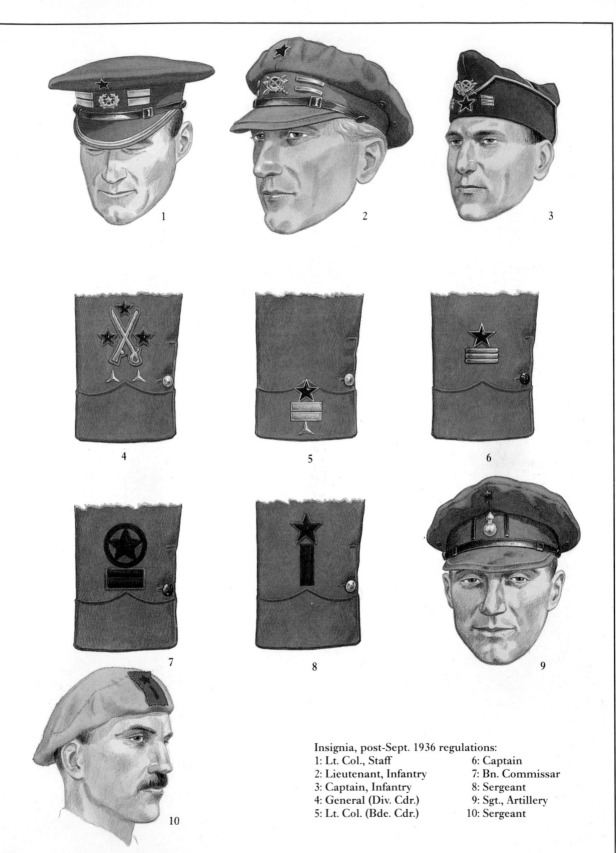

Insignia, post-Sept. 1936 regulations:
1: Lt. Col., Staff
2: Lieutenant, Infantry
3: Captain, Infantry
4: General (Div. Cdr.)
5: Lt. Col. (Bde. Cdr.)
6: Captain
7: Bn. Commissar
8: Sergeant
9: Sgt., Artillery
10: Sergeant

1: 15th International Brigade
2: Tom Mann Centuria
3: British Battalion
4: No. 1 Co., British Bn.

1

1er BATALLÓN AMERICANO

ABRAHAM LINCOLN

BRIGADA INTERNACIONAL

1: Abraham Lincoln Battalion
2: No. 3 Co., Abraham Lincoln Bn.
3: Grupo/Bn. Rakosi
4: Mackenzie-Papineau Bn.

2

TOM MOONEY

COMPANY

LINCOLN BATTALION

3

COLUMNA DE FERRO
Centuria Internacional
JSU UHP
GRUPO RAKOSI
Combatientes
Húngaros

4

CANADA'S
MACKENZIE PAPINEAU BATTALION
1837 1937
15TH BRIGADE 15TH
"Fascism shall be destroyed"

Lt. Glyn 'Taffy' Evans (left) and an unidentified volunteer of No. 1 (Major Attlee) Co., British Bn., 15th Int. Bde.; Evans wears a khaki beret with the rank insignia patch of a lieutenant, which also appears on his leather jacket. A Sam Browne belt is worn over shirt and pullover. His comrade wears a pasamontana cap and a cazadora. (IBMA)

The Nationalist Aragon Offensive
(8 March–29 July 1938)

On 9 March the Nationalists launched an offensive on a 50-mile front in Aragon with the aim of reaching the Mediterranean and cutting Republican territory in half. The 15th and 11th Int. Bdes. were rushed to the Belchite area, threatened by Gen. Solchaga's Navarrese Corps. The MacPaps were near Azuara, the Lincolns on hills to the west of Belchite, and the British on the road north to Mediana, with the 59th to their right and the Thaelmanns covering Codo. Belchite was empty when the British moved through, but on the Mediana road they met remnants of broken Republican units; then all hell broke loose as the British, 59th and Thaelmanns were attacked from the air, and by artillery and infantry. They were forced back to Belchite in an orderly retreat; five times they formed a line to hold the Nationalists at bay, and held up their advance for over a day. The British were the last Republican unit through Belchite, which fell on 10 March; the anti-tank battery had to abandon its guns there, and hence-forth they joined the infantry companies, which formed defensive lines across the Lecera road. On the 11th the Nationalists were discovered to have taken Lecera, and the British went to Vinaceite. On the 12th the British marched eastwards across country and took up positions on the Hijar-Alcaniz road. On the 13th they dug in beyond Hijar, but found that the Nationalists had taken Alcaniz in their rear, and had to strike across country again towards Caspe. Other units were also falling back all along the front.

At Caspe the remnants of several units including 15th Int. Bde. were organised for the defence of that town. The British Bn. was reduced to about 150 survivors from 500 only a few days before. On 16 March the Nationalists attacked Caspe; the fighting continued all day, but towards evening Nationalist armour rolled into Caspe, forcing the defenders out. The British withdrew towards Batea and Corbera, where reorganisation took place. Many prisoners had been lost to the Nationalists, who shot some out of hand. On 30 March the Nationalists launched another offensive to the south and north of the Ebro. The 15th Int.

Bde. were ordered to hold a line beyond Calaceite. Confusion reigned when the British mistook advancing Nationalist troops for Republicans, and large numbers were taken prisoner or killed; many more were cut off and had to infiltrate Nationalist positions and get back to Republican territory by swimming the Ebro. Some British and MacPaps regrouped near Gandesa, and this group, led by Malcolm Dunbar, held the Nationalist advance for a day in a defensible cutting. On 3 April Gandesa fell, and this group of Internationals crossed the Ebro near Cherta.

The Nationalist division of Gen. Vega finally reached the Mediterranean at Vinaroz on 15 April 1938; and Republican territory was cut in two. To the north the Nationalists had advanced to Lerida, and to the south by 29 July, they had established a line between Castellon and Segunto, although failing to take Valencia.

The Republican Ebro Offensive (July–November 1938)

The Republican offensive across the Ebro had two objectives: to relieve pressure on Valencia, and to unite the two halves of Republican territory recently divided by the Nationalists. To this purpose an 80–100,000 strong Army of the Ebro was assembled under the overall command of Juan Modesto, consisting of 5th Corps (Enrique Lister), 12th Corps (Etelvino Vega), 15th Corps (Manuel Taguena), and in reserve the 18th Corps (Jose del Barrio). In the 15th Corps were the 45th Division (including the 12th and 14th Int. Bdes.) and the 35th Division (including the 11th, 13th and 15th Int. Bdes.). There were also 70–80 field guns, 27 AA guns, 22 x T-26 tanks and four companies of armoured cars, with some 120 aircraft in support. The Republic had recently received a renewed flow of supplies over the French border, and large numbers of new I-16 Russian fighter aircraft.

The crossing began on the night of 24 July 1938, from Mequinenza to the north down to Cherta in the south, by boats and pontoons on a 50-mile front. 15th Corps crossed between Mequinenza and Fayon, and 5th Corps at 16 points between Fayon and Cherta. The 35th

Volunteer Walter Gregory of the British Bn. at La Pasionaria hospital, Murcia, after being wounded at the battle of Jarama, 1937. A native of Nottingham who had fought Moseley's Blackshirts, he served with the British Bn. as a rifleman and runner and was later promoted to lieutenant. He joined the Royal Navy in the Second World War. He is seen here wearing a typical heavy sweater, trousers with buttoned pocket flaps and alpargatos. (IBMA)

Division crossed between Flix and Mora la Nueva; first across was the reconstituted Hans Beimler Bn. of the 11th Int. Bde. (now composed of Germans, Scandinavians and Catalans). The Lincolns crossed at Flix; the MacPaps and British at Asco; and the 14th Int. Bde. at Amposta. Facing this force was one division of Legionaries and Morroccans from Yagué's Marroqui Corps. Republican 15th Corps advanced three miles from the Ebro, but in the centre Lister's 5th Corps had advanced 25 miles, almost to Gandesa. The battalions of the 15th Int. Bde. were ordered towards Corbera and Gandesa. At Corbera the 13th Int. Bde.'s flank was dominated by Moorish troops dug in on the hills; the position was cleared by the British Bn., and the 13th entered Corbera.

At Amposta the 14th Int. Bde. were held off by Gen. Lopez Bravo's division, and after 18 hours' fierce fighting and 600 dead were forced to pull back to the left bank on 26 July.

Franco's usual reaction was to pull troops quickly from other parts of the 1,100-mile front; and he moved to counter the serious Republican threat by assembling reinforcement divisions under Barron, Alfredo Glaera, Delgado Serrano, Rada, Alonso Vega, Castejon and Arias, with strong artillery and aerial support. A war of attrition began.

The British Bn. were ordered to take the fortified Hill 481 – 'The Pimple' – whose Legionary defenders were impeding the advance on Gandesa. The battalion tried to take the hill from 27 July to 2 August, some assaults being led in person by Gen. Lister, but could not get to the top, and suffered many casualties.

By 2 August the Republican advance had been brought to a standstill on a line from Fayon southwards through Corbera and Gandesa to Cherta. Each side dug in. Franco hurled in artillery and aerial attacks, and the Ebro became an artillery contest. Between 6 and 8 August Delgado Serrano's Nationalist division drove Taguena's Republicans back across the river from the Fayon–Mequineza bridgehead. During the following ten days Alonso Vega and Yagué also achieved successes. On 24 August the British Bn. relieved the Lincolns and MacPaps on Hill 666 in the Sierra Pandols, and fought off a severe attack by Alonso Vega's troops, for which they were commended. A major Nationalist counter-attack by two corps began on 3 September, and they gained some territory. Another Nationalist attack was concentrated in the Caballs-Pandols sector on 18 September, and the 15th Int. Bde. were ordered back to the front near Corbera where Republican troops had suffered heavy losses. The last action of the British, Lincolns and MacPaps took place in the Sierra Fariols near Corbera from

Commissar Walter 'Tappy' Tapsell. He wears an officer's khaki tunic and cap; with the commissar's red star, ring and bars badge. Tapsell had been leader of the Young Communist League in Britain and circulation manager of the Daily Worker. He saw action at Jarama, and commanded a group in the assaults on Mosquito Ridge at Brunete. He became Battalion Political Commissar. Tapsell went missing near Calaceite in April 1938 when the British Bn. ran into a column of Italian tanks; he was last seen firing his revolver at a tank commander. (IBMA)

22 to 24 September; they held up a Nationalist advance in this area until relieved by the 46th Division.

Franco's final massive offensive on the remaining bridgeheads in the Ebro bulge was launched with seven divisions on 30 October, with unprecedented artillery and air support. Severe fighting continued until mid-November, when the last Republican-held village fell. The Ejercito Popular had lost some 70,000 casualties, the Nationalists some 40,000. This bloodbath on the Ebro was the last fight of the International Brigades. They had fought in the thick of it, alongside the 'crack'

Gen. 'Walter' (Karol Swierczewski), extreme left, with 'La Pasionaria' (Dolores Ibbaruri) next to him after the battle of Brunete, July 1937. Walter commanded the 35th Division of the 5th Corps, which at this time included the 11th Int. Bde. and the 32nd and 108th Brigades. He is seen here with other officers reviewing the troops; all are giving the clenched fist Popular Front salute. (IBMA)

Spanish units of Lister, Modesto, El Campesino and others. Many were to remain in Spain, with the soil of Spain as their covering.

Departure

While the terrible battle of the Ebro was still raging, orders arrived for the International Brigades to withdraw. Prime Minister Juan Negrin had proposed their withdrawal under League of Nations supervision as a concession which it was hoped would be reciprocated by the Nationalists (it was not: Franco's foreign troops remained to the last, and took part in his victory parade in Madrid on 1 April 1939).

The 15th Int. Bde. and other International units of the 35th Division stood down on 24 September 1938, Spanish units under El Campesino taking over their positions. After a final parade and review at Marsa, Spanish troops – who already made up much of their strength – took the volunteers' places, and the new completely Spanish 15 Bde. moved back across the Ebro on 5 October. Another review took place on 17 October; the Internationals then moved to Ripoll to be joined by wounded from several hospitals awaiting repatriation.

On 29 October the International Brigades were called to Barcelona for a farewell parade, marching proudly down the Diagonal to the cheers and embraces of the crowd. Negrin, and the Asturias deputy Dolores Ibbaruri ('La Pasionara') expressed the Republic's gratitude in moving speeches.

By mid-January 1939 some 4,600 foreign volunteers had left Spain, to often rapturous welcomes at home; the first British contingent of 305 arrived on 7 December 1938. At least 600 remained in the ranks of Spanish units: mainly Germans, Italians, Yugoslavs, Czechs, Hungarians and others who were exiles from right-wing regimes and who had no safe home to return to. These fought on bravely until the Ebro battles ended in November, and later in the battles for Catalonia.

The Republic was finally defeated in March 1939, and surviving foreign volunteers joined the exhausted stream of Republican refugees across the Pyrenees and on to uncertain fates. Many of those captured by the Nationalists perished in captivity; some were repatriated. Many veterans of the International Brigades continued to fight fascism in the ranks of their national armies or resistance movements during the Second World War; in the words of Major Sam Wild, they fought 'on other fronts'.

Among those mostly unknown thousands of other volunteers who remained under the soil of Spain forever were some 3,000 of 10,000 French and Belgians; 2,000 of 5,000 Germans and Austrians; 600 of some 3,300 Italians; 750 of 1,500

Yugoslavs; 900 of 2,800 Americans; and 526 of 2,300 British.

THE PLATES

Given the motley range of clothing and equipment used by the Internationals, any generalisations are likely to be unsafe. The plates' subjects are reconstructed from photographs of individuals and groups, in the latter case sometimes presenting a composite of more than one figure. Given the wide range of drab khaki shades suggested by the tones in monochrome photographs, this aspect can only be guesswork. Pre-war Spanish Army uniforms seem to have favoured a greenish-drab shade not unlike, say, the 'khaki' used for Canadian battle-dress in the Second World War; French surplus would have been a browner shade; but note Alvah Bessie's comment in the Uniform section of the body text.

A1: Volunteer, Dombrowski Battalion, 11th International Brigade; Madrid, November 1936

Named after the Pole, Jaroslav Dombrowski (1838-71), a former member of the Polish Corps of Cadets at St. Petersburg who died as a leader in the defence of the Paris Commune, this unit later transferred to the 12th, 150th and 13th International Brigades. Photos show dark civilian-style clothing probably of brown corduroy and/or dark blue; whole groups wear either British Army surplus leather trench jerkins or exact copies. Spanish Army leather equipment seems to have been scarce, and many wear pale fabric ammunition bandoliers. The most common weapon was the standard Spanish Mauser rifle, M1893 or M1913, occasionally with the long M1913 bayonet. Black or very dark blue berets were ubiquitous, and remained so among many International units throughout the war.

A2: General Emilio Kleber, 11th International Brigade; Madrid, winter 1936–37

'Kleber', whose real name was Lazar or Manfred Stern, was of Romanian/Hungarian Jewish origin. An officer in the Austrian army captured by the

Volunteer Harry Dobson of the British Battalion. An unemployed miner from Blaenclydach, Wales, Dobson survived the torpedoing of the SS Barcelona on his way to Spain in June 1937, and joined the battalion in time for most actions after and including Brunete. Taken prisoner at Caspe, he escaped by knocking down his captors with his fists, boots and a tin of bully beef in a sack, and rejoined his comrades on the north bank of the Ebro by swimming the river. In the Ebro offensive he was fatally wounded during the assault on Hill 481, near Gandesa in July 1938. He is shown here wearing a serge pasamontana-style cap with buttoning flaps, a light khaki tunic and shirt. (IBMA)

Russians in 1917, he escaped, joined the Bolsheviks, and saw action against the Interventionist forces. An agent of the Comintern military section and an officer in the Red Army, he commanded the very first International units, later to form the 11th Bde., during the crucial battles for Madrid. He later commanded the Kleber Division and 45th Division, seeing much action in 1937. He was supposedly executed in the USSR during the 1938 purges. He took his nom-de-guerre from the French Revolutionary general.

He was photographed wearing the M1926 service dress of the Spanish Army over a heavy sweater, with the pre-war rank badges of a general of brigade on collar and cuff. If he wore the service cap it presumably conformed to pre-war regulations: the national arms of the Second Republic on the band, the infantry branch badge on the overhanging crown above this, and two broad gold braid strips edging the cloth-covered peak. See Plate I for insignia details.

A3: Volunteer, 11th or 12th International Brigade; Madrid, winter 1936-37

Photos and descriptions suggest that some central European volunteers wore long leather coats; the small knit cap was one of many alternatives to the black beret; and red Communist kerchiefs were popular. Dark brown corduroy was probably the most common single type of clothing. Spanish M1926 leather equipment was brown; a belt with a brass buckle plate, usually bearing the arm of service emblem, and Y-shaped braces supported three rigid cartridge boxes and, sometimes, a bayonet frog. Blankets of an infinite variety of civilian patterns were carried by volunteers throughout the war, often representing the soldier's only 'pack'.

This man carries a Spanish Mauser; during the first year the range of rifles available was to say the least varied. Tom Wintringham described 'derelict Swiss and Austrian things, Steyrs most of them', and 'odds and ends . . . clumsy bolts and sights battered to inaccuracy, a mixture of calibres . . . Ross, Remington, Japanese, Turkish, Polish, Mexican . . .'. Early in the service of the Abraham Lincoln Bn. a visitor to their commander, Merriman, found 'a sort of little wooden box with a lot of little slots in it, and sticking up in each one of these were about twelve different rounds of rifle or machine gun ammunition of different shapes and sizes', kept by Merriman as an aide memoire to the ammunition required for the range of weapons his unit had received.

B1: Lieutenant, British Battalion, 15th International Brigade, 1937

A representative example of typical company officer's uniform in the field, throughout the International Brigades; this figure is partly based on a photo of Lt. Glyn Evans of No. 1 ('Major

Volunteer Tom Jones of the Anti-Tank Battery, 15th Int. Bde. – a miner from Poncian near Wrexham, who made it to Spain with some difficulty in April 1937. Reported as having died in hospital on 9 August 1938, he was released from captivity in appalling conditions in March 1940. He had been badly wounded at the Sierra Pandols during the Ebro offensive while serving in the machine gun battalion of the 15th Corps (the ATBs had been disbanded after the Aragon retreats). He is shown here wearing a tall 'cossack' shape hat with the insignia of the artillery below the Republican red star. (IBMA)

Attlee') Co. of the British battalion. Khaki, brown or black berets were common, and a matter of personal taste; it was common for officers and senior NCOs to wear rank patches on headgear, and on the left breast. Leather zipper jackets of a wide range of 'windcheater' types were popular with all ranks. Various breeches and trousers were worn, often with laced field boots; officers frequently wore the Spanish Army 'Sam Browne'-style belt. Junior leaders carried a wide range of Astra (as here), Star, and other automatic pistols and revolvers as available. See Plate J for insignia details.

Sgt Gary McCartney (right) and two Spanish machine gunners of the British Bn., The central man displays on his *pasamontana* peak the three-point red star of the International Brigades – one of the few examples of its use on uniform which the author has come across. (IBMA)

B2: Officer, '6th February' Battalion, 15th International Brigade, 1937

Summer field dress, based on a photo of Commandant Gabriel Fort, the French commander of this Franco-Belgian unit. The '6th February' fought at Jarama and Brunete in 1937, suffering heavy casualties; from 4 August survivors were transferred to the 14th Int. Bde., ceasing to exist as a separate battalion. Gabriel Fort was blinded by a bullet wound at Brunete. He is seen here wearing a black beret without insignia, pulled forward in French civilian style; what seems to be a French Army M1935 shirt and khaki tie; French officer's pale whipcord breeches, and the popular field boots. His lack of rank insignia is not unusual. It is worth adding that wristwatches were far from universal in the 1930s; they were too expensive for most working men, and were sometimes given out as 'decorations' for good service in the International Brigades.

B3: Captain Tom Wintringham, British Battalion, 15th International Brigade, 1937

Officers sometimes acquired complete Ejercito Popular service dress uniforms, though these were worn mostly behind the lines; they are only common in photos of higher command groups. This figure is taken from a photo of the commander of the British Bn.: the open-collar M1922 tunic is worn with cuff ranking only; the standard service dress cap with insignia of the Republic, infantry branch, and rank (see under Plate J2); straight slacks, the Sam Browne. Wintringham carried the silver-topped cane in action at Jarama.

A veteran of the First World War, Tom Wintringham (1898-1949) later joined the Communist Party and was editor of *The New Left Review* and subsequently military correspondent of *The Daily Worker*. In the early days of the war he served with the Tom Mann Centuria in Barcelona, and with early medical units. He was active in recruiting British volunteers, and initially served as a machine gun instructor to the embryo units of the 15th and other brigades around Albacete. After commanding No. 2 (MG) Co. of the British unit he became the battalion's second commander, leading them at Jarama until wounded. After recuperation he helped form an officers' and NCOs' school near Albacete. He was wounded again in street fighting at Quinto, being invalided home in November 1937. During the Second World War he served as a Home Guard training instructor.

C1: Volunteer, British Battalion, 15th International Brigade; Jarama, 1937

Photos of the unit in the first half of 1937 show a mixture of what are apparently Spanish Army and

French surplus items. This Spanish four-pocket tunic was less common than the shorter blouse worn by C2; and half-breeches, probably of French origin, worn with puttees, seem to have been rather less common than long, straight, loose-cut trousers gathered at the ankle. Regulation Spanish arm of service insignia seem very seldom to have been worn on the collar by Internationals. The French Adrian helmet was more common than the also-seen Czech M1930 or the Spanish M1926 steel helmet. An infinite variety of heavy sweaters and cardigans were worn with the uniforms. This rifleman has Spanish leather equipment and boots, and the 'Mexicanski' rifle – a Remington-made Mosin-Nagant, issued in very large numbers to the Internationals.

C2: Volunteer, British Battalion, 15th International Brigade; Jarama, 1937

The *pasamontana*, a local balaclava with a vestigial peak, was very widely worn in this brigade, usually folded up into a cap comforter; rank patches were often attached to the front, as were the Republican red star badges acquired by some volunteers. The most common upper garment was a hip-length blouse, generically termed *cazadora* or 'hunting jacket'. Photos show that many were cut down from Spanish Army four-pocket tunics, falling straight to the hips without a tailored waist and retaining the tunic's pockets, cuff tabs, etc.; others were later made 'from scratch', and these details varied. Most photos of the British show loose trousers gathered at the ankle.

C3: Maxim crew, No. 2 (MG) Company, British Battalion; Jarama, 1937

This unit distinguished itself against superior numbers of Moorish and Foreign Legion troops, fighting first with rifles (since the wrong ammunition had been provided for its eight M1910 Russian Maxims) and later with its guns. The crew wear khaki blouses; one, a Spanish Army M1926 steel helmet, and the other a typical khaki beret. Their features are loosely based on those of two men who distinguished themselves in the desperate fighting of 12 February. In the helmet, Bert 'Yank' Levy fires his Maxim into the ranks of advancing enemy near Pingarron Hill. A veteran of Palestine and Jordan (1918-19), Mexico (1920-21) and Nicaragua (1926), this ex-merchant seaman from Hamilton, Ontario, survived capture by the Nationalists in Spain to serve with Wintringham as a Home Guard instructor. In the beret, Fred Copeman feeds the gun. Raised in a Suffolk workhouse, he joined the Royal Navy at 14, and was discharged after the 1931 Invergordon mutiny. An energetic member of Capt. Harry Fry's machine gun company, he was wounded at Jarama; became first second-in-command, then commander of the British Bn. in June-July 1937 and again in December; and was invalided home in April 1938.

D1: Volunteer Miles Tomalin, Anti-Tank Battery, 15th International Brigade, 1937

Photos show this typically motley costume: heavy cardigan sweater, straight Ejercito Popular trousers with vents and tapes for gathering at the ankles, and a *pasamontana*. Tomalin was a Cambridge University poet, and in his spare time edited the

Volunteer J. Brown (right) and Blas Munoz Cardenas of the British Bn. Brown wears a brown French beret, light khaki shirt, Sam Browne, dark khaki trousers gathered at the ankles and alpargatos. Cardenas wears Republican Army summer issue, apparently hardly ever received by the Internationals, except for officers. He wears an isabellino cap of green-khaki with red piping – light green-khaki shirt and breeches, brown leather leggings and boots. (IBMA)

Capt. Paddy O'Daire and Lt. George Fletcher, British Battalion. O'Daire (b. 1907 in Donegal) led the British Section, No. 2 Co., 20th Bn., 86th Mixed Bde. at Cordoba; was adjutant of No. 2 Co., British Bn. at Brunete; battalion adjutant in August 1937, and battalion CO from 26 August to 5 December 1937. He wears an unstiffened officer's cap with the gold rank bars of a captain flanking the infantry badge. Fletcher, from Crewe, had been a British Army sergeant before 1936 and used his military experience as an expert machine gunner to good effect. He too commanded the battalion, during the Ebro offensive after Sam Wild was wounded. His black beret bears the two gold bars of a lieutenant beneath the red star. (IBMA)

Anti Tanks' *Assault & Battery News*; he always carried two haversacks, accommodating his notebooks for a diary and poetry, and the recorder which he often played for the amusement of his comrades. Photos quite commonly show volunteers wearing the waistbelt of the Spanish 'Sam Browne'.

D2: British Volunteer, 1937

A composite of two men from a group photo. Lightweight summer clothing was issued to some extent; reportedly, most items had a greenish-khaki shade. Two-pocket blouses and four-pocket tunics were both seen, the latter less commonly. The cap

is interesting; of lightweight material, it has a long stiffened peak, a flap buttoning at the front, and apparently an inner pair of flaps passing over the crown. These caps, which seem to be a development of the *pasamontana* shape, occur in several photos of British volunteers.

D3: American volunteer, 1937

Another composite of two photos. The Spanish Army *gorro* or '*isabellino*' forage cap was worn widely in the Ejercito Popular; it often had the front tassel in arm-of-service colour removed, and sometimes had the front and rear crown corners pushed inside and sewn across to make a more rounded shape, but the original arm-colour piping (red for infantry) was frequently retained. Embroidered, enamel or glass red star badges were sometimes attached. Sleeveless sweaters were an issue item, and feature in many photos of Internationals, varying in detail and colour. The gaiter-trousers were the traditional *granaderos* worn for decades by the Spanish Army; more common in Nationalist ranks during the Civil War, they do feature in a few photos of the Lincolns.

Group of the largely British Anti-Tank Battery, 15th Int. Bde. at Ambite, near Madrid, possibly December 1937 immediately before the battle of Teruel. The three Soviet-made 37mm anti-tank guns, with a theoretical range of five miles, were transported in lorries and hauled by hand. Each gun had a crew of ten including ammunition carriers. Battery commanders were respectively Malcolm Dunbar, Hugh Slater, Jeff Mildwater, Otto Estensen and Arthur Nichol. Formed in May/June 1937, the ATB saw action at Jarama, Brunete, Belchite, Teruel and Aragon; it was disbanded in early 1938 during the retreat from Aragon, and its members went into the British Battalion. Artillery badges can be seen on some headgear in the photo; and note US rifle belt at right background. Miles Tamalin plays his recorder. (IBMA)

E1: Volunteer, Abraham Lincoln Battalion, 15th International Brigade; the Ebro, July 1938

Details are scarce, but it is thought that at least 80 black American volunteers served with the Lincoln and Washington Battalions. The most prominent was Capt. Oliver Law, an early member of the Tom Mooney (MG) Co., who rose to become its commissar and soon afterwards its commander between February and April 1937. He was then

British volunteers of the Anti-tank battery, 15th Int. Bde., possibly taken mid-1937. Left, Miles Ridley Tomalin (see Plate D1). Battery commander Capt. Hugh Slater, centre, wears the uniform of a captain of artillery of the Ejercito Popular Republicano. Sgt Jim Sullivan of Glasgow, right, was one of the three gun commanders at Quinto, Belchite and Fuentes de Ebro. At Belchite the No. 1 gun was fired at such a rate that the barrel burst; Sullivan's gun dominated the south side of Belchite. He wears an unstiffened hat with what appear to be sergeant's insignia either side of the artillery branch badge – see Plate J9. In the Second World War Slater served with Tom Wintringham at Osterley Park, advising on Home Guard training. (IBMA)

promoted to command the Lincoln Bn.; and in July, the short-lived George Washington Bn., until his death on Mosquito Crest at Brunete.

This volunteer wears the cotton sunhat issued to the Spanish Army since the 1920s. The *mono* overall was popular throughout the war; and Alvah Bessie recalled that he and some comrades bought new ones for the Ebro advance, glad for their pocket capacity. Traditional canvas and rope *alpargatos* espadrilles were normal summer footwear; the belt and (fairly rare) cloth-covered aluminium canteen are Peninsular Army issue items. The M1926 Degtyarev DP light machine gun had been issued to infantry units by this date.

E2: Volunteer, Abraham Lincoln Battalion, 15th International Brigade; the Ebro, July 1938
The LMG No. 2 carries its pans in a sandbag. He is one of the numbers of Hispanic (mostly Cuban and Mexican) volunteers in the American units;

and wears items seen in photos in Alvah Bessie's memoir *Men in Battle* – a short-sleeved shirt with a laced neck, and light khaki drill slacks, together with the white canvas boots associated with the Nationalist Army of Africa. The Adrian helmet was widely issued in this battalion; less frequently seen is the Spanish cavalry bandolier substituting for infantry leather equipment. The 'Mexicanski' rifle was standard issue.

E3: Volunteer, Abraham Lincoln Battalion, 15th International Brigade; summer 1937
A composite of two figures from a group possibly photographed at the time of Brunete, he wears a Czech M1930 helmet; a locally made blouse; French or US surplus khaki half-breeches, with puttees; *alpargatos*; and one of the few US M1910 web rifle belts seen in contemporary photos. Note, unusually, the gasmask; volunteers were trained in its use at Albacete, and it appears in a very few

Officers and staff of the British Bn. Standing second from right is Bob Cooney, adjutant commissar in early April 1938 and battalion commissar until September 1938. Kneeling at right in dark shirt is Sam Wild, one of the battalion commanders and one-time armourer. Several others appear to be Spanish comrades, suggesting that this photo was taken around the time of the push across the Ebro. The standing figure third from right wears a Spanish Army 'isabellino' with lieutenant's rank insignia.

photos – this appears to be a French ANP-T31 or Salvator model, slung on a long tape. His other personal equipment is slung in a blanket roll; Bessie does report some use of unspecified 'packsacks', but also that the American volunteers often discarded equipment rather than carry it (in the best American Civil War traditions . . .), sometimes even weapons and ammunition during retreats.

F1: Volunteer, Dimitrov Battalion, 15th International Brigade; Jarama, spring 1937

This 'crack' battalion of the 15th Int. Bde. was named after Georgi Mihailovitch Dimitrov (1882-1949), the Bulgarian Secretary General of the Comintern, who was active in the formation of the brigades. It was composed of Jews and Slavs from the Balkan countries, many of them refugees from Fascism. The figure is taken largely from a group photograph. He wears one of the small 'Lenin'-style caps popular on an individual basis in many of the International units (including the North American battalions). The heavy, lined winter storm jacket is one of many differing patterns worn on both sides in Spain, and known as 'Canadians'; it has sheepskin collar facing, and is single-breasted – most seem to have been double-breasted, often with whipcord loops engaging buttons or toggles. He wears the common brown corduroy uniform of the early days, and Spanish issue equipment, with a French Adrian helmet, stick grenades, and a 'Mexicanski' rifle.

F2: Volunteer, Garibaldi Battalion, 12th International Brigade; Guadalajara, March 1937

In this battle the largely Italian 12th Int. Bde. inflicted a decisive defeat on fellow Italians of the Fascist Blackshirt 'Black Flames' Division of the CTV (Italian Volunteer Corps) under Gen. Coppi, stopping an enemy advance on Madrid. Much material was abandoned, many Fascists surrendered, and the defeat had considerable political resonance in Italy. Largely based on two photographed figures, this soldier wears an M1926 Adrian helmet (Spanish helmets were also used); a heavy buttoning sweater; and the Peninsular Army's old double-breasted tabardo overjacket, phased out in c.1930 but seen in many Civil War photographs. Note the forward-buttoning flaps over the slash pockets of the straight, loose trousers. On his Spanish leather equipment he carries two cylindrical pouches for the Lafitte hand grenade; these seem rarely to have been available, and other photos show white-metal grenades tied to the shoulder braces or belt with strips of rag.

F3: Volunteer, Rakosi Battalion, 13th International Brigade, 1938

A group photo reproduced in this book shows a variety of kit, worn mostly with Spanish steel M1926 helmets and uniforms. This figure wears what appears to be the British trench jerkin over the Peninsular Army four-pocket tunic and straight trousers, the latter gathered into boots with an integral two-buckle gaiter flap – these are shown in the photograph, but seem generally to have been a late and fairly rare issue on both sides. Leather equipment seems to be assembled from basic M1926 belt and braces, and the small ammunition pouches (including a pair worn on the braces) normally seen in photos of the Nationalists' Moroccan and Foreign Legion infantry. The rifle is the US P17. Note field dressing taped to a buttonhole – these were fairly rare. All in all, this Central European and Balkan unit gives a notably modern, well-equipped impression.

G1: Captain Edward C. Smith, MacKenzie-Papineau Battalion, 15th International Brigade; La Muela, Teruel, January 1938

The Republican Teruel offensive, conducted in deep snow and freezing temperatures, was initially a wholly Spanish operation; but the 11th and 15th Int. Bdes. were later brought in to stem the Nationalist counter-offensive. Smith, a Marxist journalist from Toronto with considerable military experience, commanded the George Washington Bn.'s No. 2 Co. at Brunete, suffering a shattered left hand. He later became the fifth CO of the 'MacPaps', and their longest-serving commander. Described as 'like a beefy college professor in uniform', he led his HQ staff in throwing back an enemy cavalry attack at Teruel, and at Segura de Los Banos he again used his fighting experience to good effect. Promoted major, he was hospitalised through exhaustion after the Aragon retreats, but remained in Spain until the final departure of the Internationals. He was photographed at Teruel wearing a *pasamontana* with a 'bobble' top – common in this unit – complete with rank patch; and the Spanish collared (and often hooded) *capote-manta*, a generously cut woollen cloth poncho often issued in place of a greatcoat. At freezing Teruel he wears both.

G2: Volunteer, MacKenzie-Papineau Battalion, 15th International Brigade; Teruel, January 1938

A composite from a photo of two of the 'Fighting Canucks' in the Teruel trenches, he wears an Adrian helmet camouflaged with paint or pale clay; a blanket arranged poncho-fashion over his (French?) greatcoat and under Spanish leather equipment, and a second blanket in a roll; half-

No. 1 (Major Attlee) Co., British Bn., 15th Int. Bde., 35th Div. on the Marsa road, near Mora de Nova, in training before the battle of the Ebro, July 1938. Most seem to be wearing light khaki uniform, a few wear 'isabellino' caps. The rifles are 'Mexicanskis'; one volunteer carries a Degtyarev DP light machine gun, indicating that by the time of the Ebro the infantry companies included machine guns as well as rifles. (IBMA)

breeches, and puttees. A small 'ditty bag' for personal kit is tied to his belt, as is a pocket knife. His 'Mexicanski' is carried with the bayonet fixed but reversed.

G3: Volunteer, MacKenzie-Papineau Battalion, 15th International Brigade; Teruel, January 1938

Several members of the North American battalions were photographed wearing the very large French Chasseur-style beret. Alvah Bessie records that the 'MacPaps' had Czech light machine guns by summer 1938, these may already have been available in Aragon; the only possible model would be the famous ZB26/30 series. The haversack is US Army surplus, photographed in Spain as early as 1936.

H1: Medical volunteer, Barcelona, 1937

One of a group of British volunteers who travelled to Spain to work as ambulance drivers was photographed wearing this typical outfit. Black and brown zipper jackets were thought to be practical (and by some idealists, probably romantic, too). Civilian riding breeches are worn with a pair of

Officers of the British Bn. on Hill 481 – since named the Cota del Muerte ('Hill of Death') – near Gandesa in July 1938 during the Ebro offensive. Standing right to left: Capt. Sam Wild (Bn. CO), leaning against tree; Lt. Cipriano (CO, Spanish Co.), hand on leg; Capt. Paddy O'Daire (ex-Bn. CO); Alan Gilchrist (ex anti-tank battery/Commissar No. 1 Co.); Bob Cooney (Bn. Commissar), without belt; Maj. Jose Antonio Valledor (Spanish/Asturian CO of 15th Bde.), with map. Sitting in front: Capt. George Fletcher (ex-Bn. CO) with Peter Kerrigan, a base Commissar, behind him. Most by this time are wearing officer's caps and Ejercito Popular insignia, although a few older berets from Jarama days are still in evidence; two wear the 'isabellino' in green-khaki with red piping. Most wear light khaki shirts and slightly darker khaki trousers, although Cooney has an officer's khaki tunic and Wild a short jacket (open at the front) with Captain's rank insignia on his left breast. The battalion by this time was a largely Spanish unit. (IBMA/BA)

field boots, with zip fasteners rather than lacing.

H2: Doctor, Canadian Blood Transfusion Unit; Madrid, 1937

A well-known photo shows Drs. Norman Bethune, Henning Dorensen and Hazen Size with their Ford stationwagon ambulance. Bethune ran this small unit from early 1937 to July, mainly in an instructional role, though they did valuable service as ambulance drivers at the siege of Malaga. Blood transfusion from stored plasma was then in its infancy, and Bethune believed it more valuable to spread this technique rather than serving as just another surgeon alongside Spanish colleagues. He was to die as a volunteer doctor with the Chinese army fighting the Japanese in November 1939. The volunteers assembled their own outfits of black beret, dark blue overalls with yellow 'Canada' shoulder titles, and red cross badges – the latter was subsequently replaced by the badge of the Sanidad Militar.

H3: Stretcher bearer, Sanidad Militar, Madrid 1936

From a photograph reproduced in this book. He wears Peninsular Army tunic (with wreathed Maltese cross branch badges on the collar), trousers, puttees and boots. Note the zipped civilian shirt/sweaters worn under the tunic – the zip fastener was clearly one of the most appreciated trivia of the late 1930s. The Maltese cross is repeated on the Spanish M1926 helmet. He carries field dressings.

I: Insignia, pre-September 1936 regulations

In that month the Republic adopted a new scheme of rank insignia. Given the difficulties experienced by the Internationals in acquiring serviceable weapons, correct insignia probably came a long way down their list of priorities; but during 1937 most officers and senior NCOs, at least, would have acquired them. Pre-war Peninsular Army insignia would certainly have been seen during the first year of the war, and they are illustrated in this plate.

I1 & I6: Capitan, Infantry

The three junior officer ranks were identified by one, two and three six-pointed stars, worn in a line on the service cap band and in a triangle above the cuff on the tunic sleeve. Officers' stars were also supposed to be worn in a row on a rectangular cloth patch on the left breast of field uniforms. On the cap the arm-of-service badge – for the infantry, a gold buglehorn, with crossed rifle and sword –

Capt. (later Maj.) Malcolm Dunbar (1912-1963) in the uniform of the Chief of Staff of the 15th Int. Bde., in which position he helped plan the successful crossing of the Ebro. Dunbar, always immaculate, wears a khaki 'isabellino' with (possibly) the blue piping of the Estado Mayor, captain's bars below a red star, and the emblem of the Estado Mayor – a star surrounded by laurels – which is also worn on each tunic lapel.

was pinned to the centre front of the crown. Note the broad, stiffened shape of the crown, characteristic of Spanish Army officers' caps, and the prominent stitched seam on the cloth-covered peak.

I2: Other Ranks, Engineers

The Other Ranks' service cap, quite widely worn by NCOs and even privates early in the war, was basically similar though with a smaller, unstiffened crown. The arm-of-service badge – here the silver tower of the Engineers – was worn on the band.

I3 & I4: General de Division, de Brigada

The general officers' ranking was worn on the tunic collar and cuff – see Plate A2. The cap peak bore double gold edge braid, and its band the gold coat of arms of the Second Republic (as central motif, Plate K1).

Farewell parade of the International Brigades in the Diagonal, Barcelona, Saturday 29 October 1938. An estimated 300,000 women and children (the men were still at the front) expressed with tears, flowers and embraces their feelings towards the Brigades. Prime Minister Juan Negrin and Dolores Ibbaruri ('La Pasionaria') expressed the gratitude of the Republic. The Brigaders marched past President Manuel Azana, still with the dirt of the battlefields on them and it was said that 'they learned to fight before they learned to march'. In this photograph various banners of the Brigades are being paraded. (IBMA)

I5: Coronel

The three field ranks wore one, two and three gold eight-pointed stars on the cap band and on the cuff. The cap peak had one gold braid round the edge.

I7: Brigada

This patch identified the senior NCO rank.

I8: Sargento

Three gold diagonals on the forearms marked the sergeant; the cabo (corporal) had the same bars in red, divided by black.

J: Insignia, post-September 1936 regulations

J1: Teniente-coronel, Staff

The officers' cap was basically unchanged, retaining the double and (as here) single gold braids on the peak for generals and field ranks. The arm-of-service badge moved down to the centre front of the band; with the Republican red enamel star pinned to the crown. Exact rank was indicated by gold bars on each side of the arm-of-service badge: for the three field ranks, one, two or three thick bars. The staff badge was a wreathed star. This cap is from a portrait photo of Lt. Col. Vladimir Copic, Yugoslav commander of 15th International Brigade.

J2: Teniente, Infantry

The junior officers' insignia differed only in the lack of peak braid, and the narrow gold bars each side of the arm badge – here the two of a lieutenant. The crushed, faded 'operational' appearance is taken from the portrait photo of Capt. Paddy O'Daire reproduced in this book, and seems to have been not untypical among the Internationals.

J3: Capitan, Infantry

The officers' *gorro* sidecap of the Peninsular Army was often retained with new insignia by Spanish officers, though the tassel was frequently removed. Officers' piping was double, in arm-colour and gold or silver. This example, from a photo of Capt. Nogueras of the Spanish 24th Bn., 15th Int. Bde., in fact has non-regulation insignia: the infantry badge is attached to the upper front, and the star below it between small triple rank bars – the reverse of the normal practice on service caps. The sidecap seldom bore the arm-of-service badge at all, usually receiving the same star-and-bars patch as worn on berets and jackets.

J4: General (Division Commander)

The Republic adopted a single general officer rank,

identified by this insignia of three red stars and crossed sword and baton, worn above the cuff. The level of operational command – if any – was marked by added silver three-point command stars below the ranking, here the pair of a divisional commander. Few Internationals commanded divisions, but exceptions were:

Gen. Lukacs (Mata Zalka Kemeny, a Hungarian former officer of the Austrian Army and the Red Army; led 12th Int. Bde., Madrid, 1936; led Division Lukacs briefly, Dec. 1936-Jan. 1937; led 12th Int. Bde. at Jarama, Guadalajara, Brunete, and Huesca, where he was killed). *Gen. Walter* (Karol Swierczewski, a Polish Red Army officer; led 14th Int. Bde., Dec. 1936-Feb. 1937; led Division A at Jarama; led 35th Div., May 1937-May 1938; subsequently Minister of Defence in Communist Poland, and killed by Ukrainian partisans in 1947). *Gen. Kleber* (Lazar Stern – see Plate A2 – led 45th Div. at various times, as did the German *Col. Hans*). Republican generals retained the cap with double peak braids, and the arms of the Second Republic on the band, with an enamel or glass red star on the front of the crown.

J5: Teniente-coronel (Brigade Commander)
Field officers wore – cf. J1 – one, two or three thick gold bars, beneath the red star, on the cuff itself. As with all officer ranks, exactly the same display was often worn as a single patch on the left chest of field clothing. A single silver three-pointed star marked a brigade command. Officers wore arm-of-service badges on tunic lapels, though photos of Internationals often show them absent.

J6: Capitan
Junior officers wore ranking above the cuff: one, two and three narrow gold bars for Alfárez, Teniente and Capitan, all beneath the red star. Photos suggest that stars were sometimes pin-on enamelled metal, sometimes embroidered; rank bars seem usually to have been gold braid, but some metal pin-on examples may have been used.

J7: Commissario de Battalion
Political commissars wore a red cloth star in a circle, above two red bars (for battalion commissars) or one red bar (for company commissars). These were displayed above the cuff; some photos show them repeated on the crown and band respectively of the service dress cap; they were often worn as a patch on the front of field headgear and the left chest of field clothing. It should be pointed out that among the Internationals commissars often distinguished themselves in action, many losing their lives in battle at the head of their troops.

J8: Sargento
The forearm ranking was a red star, without yellow edging, above a vertical red bar with (or in practice, often without) yellow edging. The *cabo* ranking was a short, thick inverted Vee in red braid; it was hardly ever seen in practice. Corporals tended to be made up in the field, and often did not survive in the rank long enough to bother about insignia.

J9: Sargento, Artillery
On the service dress cap, a popular item often worn in the field by senior NCOs, the red star (officially without edging) appeared above the arm-of-service badge, which was flanked by red vertical bars.

J10: Sargento
On a typical variation of the khaki beret, the ranking is worn as an embroidered patch, as also worn on the left chest of field clothing. The senior NCO or Brigada wore a star above two vertical red bars.

Insignia of the Brigadas Internacionales
The decree of 23 September 1937 instituted a three-point red star as the badge of the International Brigades. This was to be worn on the right chest of the shirt or jacket 2 cm above the pocket. A few photos show it worn on the right arm (e.g. by Luigi Longo, Inspector General of the Brigades), or on the cap (as in a photo reproduced in this book). However, it was rarely seen as a badge on uniform, and saw its widest use on posters and banners. Today it is used by the International Brigade Association.

K1: Speculative banner of the 15th International Brigade

It is known that the International Brigades were presented with banners in the Calderon Theatre, Madrid. This partly speculative reconstruction is based on the known pattern of other brigades of the Ejercito Popular, and on a blurred photograph of that occasion. The arms of the second republic, and the divisional and brigade titles, are displayed on the red, gold and purple tricolour of the Republic.

K2: Tom Mann Centuria, 1936

The banner is shown in a photo (reproduced elsewhere in this book) taken at the Karl Marx Barracks, Barcelona, in September 1936. The colours are speculative. The legend translates as 'Tom Mann English Anti-Fascist Centuria – Proletarian Discipline will defeat Fascism'. Tom Mann (1856-1941) was an English trade unionist.

K3: British Battalion (57th Bn.), 15th International Brigade

A replica of this banner, which was taken into action at Teruel and Segura de Los Banos, and whose design is confirmed by photographs, is preserved by the International Brigade Association; it now bears the battalion's battle honours up to the Ebro. Photos show the original to have been of relatively small size, perhaps five by four feet.

K4: No. 1 ('Major Attlee') Company, British Battalion

No. 1 Company had fought under the command of George Nathan on the Cordoba front, with 14th Int. Bde., before the survivors were incorporated into 15th Int. Bde.; the banner was made for the company following a visit to the unit by Maj. Clement Attlee, leader of the British Labour Party (and Prime Minister 1945-51), on 6 December 1937 at Mondejar, shortly before their departure for the Teruel campaign.

L1: Abraham Lincoln Battalion (58th Bn.), 15th International Brigade

The colours are speculative. This banner was paraded in Barcelona in early January 1937 by the first large group of American recruits who sailed from New York to Le Havre on the SS *Normandie*; strictly, they had yet to be incorporated into the brigade, but the banner no doubt accompanied them. We reconstruct its colours to match the known blue of the battalion's machine gun company (L2), but the ground may possibly have been red.

L2: No. 3 ('Tom Mooney') Company, Abraham Lincoln Battalion

The battalion's machine gun company is known to have had this banner at the battle of Jarama, where it was photographed. Tom Mooney was an American trade unionist who, in 1937, was serving a life sentence in Alcatraz Federal Prison.

L3: Grupo Rakosi

This early Hungarian unit of international volunteers was later incorporated as the Rakosi Bn. (51st), servicing first with the 150th and later with the 13th International Brigade. A photo reproduced in this book shows that the banner was retained. The wording may be translated as: 'Iron Column, International Century, United Socialist Youth, Union of Proletarian Brothers, Rakosi Group, Hungarian Fighters'. The JSU was part of the United Socialist Party of Catalonia, the PSUC.

L4: MacKenzie-Papineau Battalion (60th Bn.), 15th International Brigade

The battalion, named after two republican activists of 1837, was formed in July 1937. Its core were Canadians who had been fighting in the ranks of the Abraham Lincoln Bn. and the new unit also contained many Americans, as well as Anglo-Saxon, Finnish and Ukrainian Canadians. The colours of the banner are, again, partly speculative, but its design is clearly shown in a photograph of the Finnish machine gun company; it appears to be about six feet long.

Select Bibliography

F. Borkenau, *The Spanish Cockpit* (London, 1937)

Bob Cordery, *La Ultima Cruzada – A Wargamer's Guide to the Spanish Civil War* (Partizan Press, 1989)

R. Fraser, *Blood of Spain* (Penguin, 1981)

J. Tisa (ed.), *The Pallette & the Flame* (Collets, 1980)

H. Thomas, *The Spanish Civil War*

A. Castells, *Las Brigadas Internacionales de la Guerra de Espana* (Horas de Espana, Barcelona, 1974)

F. Ryan (ed.), *The Book of the XV Brigade* (1939) (F Graham - 1975)

Bill Alexander, *British Volunteers for Liberty* (Lawrence & Wishart, 1982)

Bill Alexander, *No to Franco – the Struggle Never Stopped, 1939–1975* (June, 1992)

Bob Clark, *No Boots on my Feet* (Students Bookshops, 1984)

F. Copeman, *Reason in Revolt* (Blandford Press, 1948)

J. A. Cornford, *Memorial Volume* (ed. P. Sloan) (Cape, 1938)

J. Coward, *Escape From the Dead* (Daily Worker pamphlet, 1940?)

Ralph Fox, *A Writer in Arms* (Lawrence & Wishart, 1937)

H. Francis, *Miners Against Fascism* (Lawrence & Wishart, 1984)

W. Gregory, *The Shallow Grave* (Gollancz, 1986)

E. Romilly, *Boadilla* (London, 1937)

W. Rust, *Britons in Spain* (Gollancz, 1939)

J. Sommerfield, *Volunteer in Spain* (London, 1937)

Tom Wintringham, *English Captain* (Faber, 1939)

Alvah Bessie, *Men in Battle* (New York, Chas. Scribners, 1939)

A. Landis, *The Abraham Lincoln Brigade* (Citadel, 1967)

Edwin Rolfe, *The Lincoln Battalion* (New York, 1939)

V. Hoar, *The MacKenzie-Papineau Battalion* (Canada: Copp Clark, 1969)

J. M. Bueno, *Uniformes Militares en color de la Guerra Civil Española* (Madrid, 1971)

Raymond Carr, *Images of the Spanish Civil War* (Guild, 1986)

Ian MacDougal (ed.), *Voices from the Spanish Civil War* (Polygon, 1986)

Manuel Tunon de Lara, *La Battalla de Teruel* (Castillas turolenses, 1986)

Patrick Turnbull & Jeffery Burn, *The Spanish Civil War 1936-39*, Osprey MAA 74 (London, 1978)

Jack Gibbs, *The Spanish Civil War* (Benn, 1973)

David Mitchell, *The Spanish Civil War* (Granada, 1982)

Jose Maria Armero & Manuel Gonzalez, 'Armas y Pertrechos de la Guerra Española', *Historia* 16 (1981)

C. A. Norman, articles in *Tradition* magazine nos 66 & 67

George Hills, *The Battle for Madrid* (Vantage Books, 1976)

Michael Alpert, El Ejército Republicano en la Guerra Civil (Reading University Thesis/Madrid, Siglo XXI dede Espana, 1989)

German Democratic Republic, *'Der Kriegen in Spanien'*

Notes sur les planches en couleur

Remarque Les planches sont inspirées à partir de photographies et des descriptions de témoins mais les couleurs exactes, dans de nombreux cas, sont seulement spéculatives. Les uniformes de l'armée espagnole d'avant 1936 sont portés, mais de nombreux volontaires reçurent un mélange d'articles espagnols, de surplus étrangers et de vêtements civils.

A1 Les photos montrent des vêtements en velours côtelé bleu foncé et marron, avec des pourpoints en cuir de type britannique et les munitions sont portées surtout dans de simples bandoulières à cartouches en coton. La plupart des fusils étaient des Mausers espagnols. A2 Cet agent Cominterm, à la tête des premiers Internationaux qui défendirent Madrid, porte un uniforme d'officier et des insignes d'avant 1936. La tunique de modèle 1926 avait un col fermé. A3 Les photos et les descriptions confirment le port de longs manteaux de cuir et d'équipement espagnol en cuir de 1926 avec béret noir et divers bonnets tricotés.

B1 Représentant typique d'officier volontaire étranger en tenue de campagne. Insignes de rang républicain sur le béret, la très populaire veste de cuir à fermeture éclair 'windcheater' dont on voyait des variations infinies. Ceinture espagnole 'Sam Browne', pistolet Astra, et les très populaires bottines lacées que de nombreux volontaires achetèrent. B2 Tenue de campagne d'été portée sur une photo par le Cdt. Gabriel Fort, qui perdit la vue à Brunete à la tête de ce bataillon. B3 Tenue de service espagnole de modèle 1922 que portaient certains officiers aux arrières avec insignes de rang républicain de capitaine sur la manchette et de capitaine d'infanterie sur la casquette. Certains portaient des badges d'armes au col. Wintringham, blessé à la tête du bataillon britannique, portait seulement une canne à Jarama.

C1 Les casques Adrian étaient le type le plus couramment utilisé dans la plupart des unités Internationales, parallèlement a des casques tchèques, portugais et soviétiques et de nombreux casques espagnols. La tunique espagnole guerra à quatre poches était utilisée mais pas aussi souvent que les blouses raccourcies. Les demi-culottes avec bandes molletières était moins courantes que le pantalon long et ample attaché à la cheville. Matériel de cuir espagnol, fusil 'Mexicanski' (Mozin-Nagant fabriqué par Remington). C2 Le très courant pasamontana, un passe-montagne tricoté qui se repliait pour former un bonnet (et qui portait souvent une étoile rouge et/ou des insignes de rang) et la cazadora ou

Farbtafeln

Anmerkung: Die Bildtafeln wurden nach Fotos und nach einigen Augenzeugen-Berichten rekonstruiert; die genauen Farben sind jedoch in vielen Fällen nur spekulativer Natur. Obwohl auch einige Uniformstücke der spanischen Armee aus der Zeit vor 1936 getragen wurden, erhielten die Freiwilligen eine bunte Zusammenstellung spanischer, ausländischer und ziviler Kleidungsstücke.

A1 Fotos zeigen dunkelblaue und dunkelbraune Cord-Kleidungsstücke, mit Lederjacken nach britischer Art; die Munition wurde meistens in einfachen Baumwoll-Patronengurten mitgetragen. Es gab meistens spanische Mausergewehre. A2 Dieser Komintern-Agent der die ersten Internationalen bei der Verteidigung von Madrid befehligte, trägt die Uniform und Insignien eines Generals vor 1936; die Bluse von 1926 hat einen geschlossenen Kragen. A3 Fotos und Beschreibungen bestätigen lange Ledermäntel und komplette spanische Lederausrüstung von 1926, schwarze Baskenmützen oder verschiedene Wollkappen.

B1 Typischer ausländischer Freiwilligen-Offizier in Felduniform. Republikanische Rangabzeichen an der Mütze; die sehr populäre, zivile Lederwindjacke mit Zipp, von der es unzählige Versionen gab; spanischer "Sam Browne"-Gürtel, Astra-Pistole und die sehr beliebten Schnürstiefel, die sie viele Freiwillige kauften. B2 Sommer-Felduniform, in diesem Foto von Kommandant Gabriel Fort getragen, der bei Brunete als Führer dieses Bataillons durch eine Verletzung erblindete. B3 Spanische Galauniform von 1922, von manchen Offizieren hinter der Front getragen, mit republikanischen Hauptmanns-Rangabzeichen an der Manschette und dem infanterie-Hauptmanns auf der Kappe. Manche trugen Waffengattungs-Abzeichen auf dem Kragen. Wintringham, der bei Führung eines britischen Bataillons verwundet wurde, trug bei Jarama nur einen Stock.

C1 Adrian-Helme waren bei den meisten Einheiten der Internationalen am häufigsten, zusammen mit tschechischen, portugiesischen und vielen spanischen Helmen. Die spanische Guerra-Bluse mit vier Taschen wurde ebenfalls ausgegeben, aber nicht so häufig wie die verkürzten Blusen; die Halbbreeches mit Wickelgamaschen waren weniger häufig als lange, lose, am Knöchel zusammengebundene Hosen. Spanische Lederausrüstung; "Mexicanski"-Gewehr – ein von Remington gebautes Modell Mosin-Nagant. C2 Das sehr weit verbreit-

blouse courante, coupée au niveau de la tunique ou faite sur mesure. C3 Les huit Maxims de cette compagnie repoussèrent les attaques ennemies le 12 fév rier malgré de lourdes pertes républicaines et la fourniture initiale des mauvaises munitions. Les casques espagnols et différents bérets khaki étaient relativement courants parmi les Internationaux.

D1 La batterie de la brigade antichars (fusils soviétiques 37mm) était principalement britannique. Cette figure est inspirée d'une photographie du volontaire Miles Tomalin. D2 Inspiré d'une photographie de volontaires britanniques en uniforme d'été léger. Notez la casquette intéressante. D3 Bonnet espagnol ou gorro sans son pompon et les pointes cousues, avec badge étoile rajouté. Les pullovers sans manches étaient parmi les articles distribués. Le pantalon à guêtres granadero n'était pas courant mais on le voyait parfois.

E1 Environ 80 volontaires noirs servirent dans les unités américaines avec des blancs, des cubains, mexicains, philippins etc. Il porte l'ancien chapeau de soleil de l'armée espagnole, le pardessus mono très courant comme uniforme de combat d'été ainsi que les espadrilles en tissu très courantes nommées alpargatas. Ceinture et gourde de l'armée espagnole et mitraillette légère DP soviétique. E2 Casque Adrian et vêtements d'été inspirés de photographies de cette unité, y compris les bottes en tissu comme celles portées par les troupes nationalistes de l'armée africaine. On voyait quelquefois des bandoulières à cartouches de cavalerie parmi les troupes d'infanterie. Il porte des munitions pour le DP. E3 Inspiré d'une photographie – casque tchèque M1930, blouse fabriquée sur place, demi-culotte provenant sans doute de surplus américains, ceinture US M1910, fusil 'Mexicanski' et masque à gaz français. Des couvertures de type civil était le 'barda' que les Internationaux portaient le plus souvent.

F1 Les photographies montrent des casquettes de type 'Lénine' de temps en temps dans de nombreuses unités. La canadienne était appréciée de ceux qui pouvaient s'en procurer une et les vêtements en velours côtelé marron étaient courants. F2 Il porte l'ancienne veste tabardo de l'armée espagnole et un pantalon droit avec des revers de poche boutonnés. Notez les poches cylindriques destinées aux grenades Lafitte. F3 Uniforme et casque espagnols. Matériel cuir espagnol avec petites poches comme l'Armée africaine. Pourpoint de type britannique, rares bottes avec revers à boucle, fusil américain P17.

G1 Les photographies montrent des canadiens portant le pasamontana avec un pompon de laine au sommet. Le capote-manta, avec un grand col et souvent une capuche, remplaçait le manteau, mais ce commandant de bataillon porte les deux. Notez les insignes de rang sur le couvre-chef. G2 Tenue d'hiver typique dans les tranchées. G3 On voit de grands bérets français sur certaines photos. On dit que ce bataillon utilisa la mitraillette légère tchèque ZB26/30. Notez également le sac à dos des surplus américains.

H1 Vêtements typiques de volontaire civil à cette période. H2 Inspiré de photographies des trois docteurs canadiens de ce groupe de volontaires. H3 Uniforme de l'armée espagnole avec croix maltaise du service médical sur le casque.

I Avant septembre 1936, tous les officiers (et pendant de nombreux mois par la suite beaucoup d'entre eux) portaient des insignes de rang et de branche de l'armée péninsulaire. Sur la casquette de service les officiers portaient des badges d'armes sur la calotte et le rang sur le ruban. Pour les échelons en dessous il s'agissait de une, deux et trois étoiles dorées à six branches, répétées au dessus de la manchette. Pour les rangs supérieurs il y avait une, deux et trois étoiles dorées à huit branches sur le ruban de la casquette et sur la manchette. La visière de leur casquette était bordée de galon doré. Les généraux portaient les armoiries de la 2nde République sur la bande de leur casquette et deux galons dorés sur la visière. Pour avoir plus de détails sur chaque rang, voir les légendes en anglais.

J Les insignes réglementaires d'après septembre 1936. La casquette des officiers portait le même galon doré pour les rangs supérieurs et les rangs ordinaires. Les officiers supérieurs avaient une, deux et trois barres épaisses de chaque côté du badge d'armes sur la bande, les officiers de compagnie avaient une, deux et trois barres dorées minces. Tous portaient l'étoile républicaine rouge sur la calotte. Les insignes de rang portées sur la manche étaient comme le montre l'illustration. Voir les légendes en anglais pour chaque rang. J3 indique, inspiré d'une photographie, un arrangement non standard des insignes sur le gorro. J4, J5 montrent les étoiles argentées à trois branches qui indiquent le commandement d'une division ou brigade porté en dessous du rang normal. La République n'avait qu'un rang d'officier général. J9 :montre les barres verticales rouges d'un sergent de chaque côté du badge d'armes. J10 un écusson de rang typique sur le béret d'un sergent.

K1 Spéculatif, inspiré d'un modèle connu utilisé par d'autres brigades. K2 Inspiré d'une photographie. Les couleurs sont spéculatives. K3 Cet arrangement est confirmé par des photos. Une réplique est conservée. Le drapeau fut emmené au front à Teruel. K4 Inspiré de photographies. Ce drapeau fut adopté après la visite que fit Clement Attlee, qui devint par la suite Premier Ministre britannique, à cette unité en sa capacité de chef du Parti travailliste en décembre 1937.

L1 Inspiré d'une photographie. Les couleurs sont inspirées des couleurs connues de L2 La compagnie de mitraillettes de ce bataillon avait ce drapeau à Jarama. L3 Photographié porté par les premiers Grupo, puis le Bataillon, qui se battit avec la 150ème et la 13ème Brigade. L4 Inspiré d'une photographie; les couleurs sont imaginées.

ete Pasamontana, ein gestrickter, wollener Kopfschützer, in die Kappe gefaltet (und oft mit rotem Stern und/oder Rangabzeichen), sowie die übliche Cazadora-Bluse, gekürzt von der Uniformbluse oder direkt so angefertigt. C3 Die acht Maxim-MGs dieser Kompanie schlugen am 12. Februar Feindangriffe trotz schwerer Verluste und der ursprünglich ausgegebenen falschen Munition zurück. Spanische Helme und verschiedene Khaki-Baskenmützen waren bei der Internationalen Brigade ziemlich verbreitet.

D1 Die Panzerabwehr-Batterie (sowjetische 37mm-Kanonen) hatte meist britische Kanoniere; diese Figur ist nach einem Foto des Freiwilligen Miles Tomalin. D2 Nach dem Foto britischer Freiwilliger in leichten Sommeruniformen; siehe interessante Kappe. D3 Spanisches Gorro-Käppi mit abgenommener Quaste, Spitzen niedergenäht; zusätzliches Sternabzeichen. Ärmellose Pullover wurden offiziell ausgegeben. Die Granadero-Gamaschenhose war nicht häufig, aber doch gelegentlich zu sehen.

E1 In den amerikanischen Einheiten dienten etwa 80 schwarze Freiwillige – neben Weißen, Kubanern, Mexikanern, Filipinos usw. Er trägt den alten Hut der spanischen Armee; der beliebte Mono-Overall als Sommer-Kampfuniform sowie die ganz gewöhnlichen Alpargatos, Segeltuchsandalen. Spanischer Armeegürtel und Wasserflasche; leichtes sowjetisches DP-Maschinengewehr. E2 Adrian-Helm, Sommerkleidung nach Fotos dieser Einheit, inkl. Segeltuchstiefel, wie sie die nationalistischen Truppen der afrikanischen Armee trugen. Kavallerie-Bandoliers wurden gelegentlich auch bei der Infanterie gesehen. Er trägt Munition für das DP-MG. E3 Nach einem Foto – tschechischer Helm M1930, lokal hergestellte Bluse, Halbbreeches, wahrscheinlich US-Armeeüberschuß, US-Gürtel M1910, "Mexicanski"-Gewehr und französische Gasmaske. Die üblichsten Ranzen der Intenationalen Brigade waren aus Decken mit Zivilmustern.

F1 Fotos zeigen in vielen Einheiten gelegentlich Kappen à la Lenin; die schwere Sturmjacke ("Canadian") war sehr beliebt, wenn man sie bekommen konnte; braune Cord-Kleidung war üblich. F2 Er trägt die alte spanische Tabardo-Armeejacke und gerade Hose mit zuknöpfbaren Hosentaschen. Siehe zylindrische Taschen für Lafitte-Granaten. F3 Uniform und Helm spanisch; spanische Ledergurte, mit kleinen Taschen wie die der afrikanischen Armee; Westen britischer Art; seltene Stiefel mit Knöchelschnallen; amerikanisches P17-Gewehr.

G1 Fotos zeigen Kanadier mit Pasamontana-Kopfschützer mit Wollkugel oben. Der Capote-Manta mit breitem Kragen und oft auch mit Kapuze war ein Ersatz für den langen Armeemantel, obwohl dieser Bataillonskommandant beides trägt. Siehe Rangabzeichen an der Kopfbedeckung. G2 Typische Winterkleidung in den Schützengräben. G3 Große französische Mützen sind auf vielen Fotos zu sehen. Das tschechische Leicht-MG ZB26/30 soll bei diesem Bataillon gesehen worden sein; siehe auch Ranzen aus US-Überschuß.

H1 Typische Zivilkleidung für Freiwillige in dieser Periode. H2 Von Fotos der drei kanadischen Ärzte dieser Freiwilligen-Einheit. H3 Spanische Armeeuniform, mit Malteserkreuz des Sanitätsdienstes auf dem Helm.

I Vor dem September 1936 – und für viele Monate danach – trugen viele Offiziere wenn überhaupt Rang- und Einheitsabzeichen der Halbinsel- Armee. Auf der Kappenkrone der Ausgehuniform trugen Offiziere Waffengattungsabzeichen, und die Rangabzeichen am Kappenband; das waren für Subalternoffiziere ein, zwei oder drei sechsspitzige Goldsterne auf Kappe und über der Manschette, für höhere Offiziere ein, zwei oder drei achtspitzige Goldsterne auf Kappenband und Manschette; ihre Kappenschirme waren mit Goldlitze eingefaßt. Generale trugen Wappen der 2. Republik auf dem Kappenband sowie zwei Goldeinfassungen am Schirm. Siehe englischen Bildtext für die einzelnen Ränge.

J Die vorschriftsmäßigen Insignien nach September 1936. Offizierskappen zeigten dieselben Goldlitzen für Feldoffiziere und Generalsränge. Feldoffiziere trugen ein, zwei oder drei breite Goldstreifen zu jeder Seite des Waffengattungsabzeichens auf dem Kappenband, Subalternoffiziere ein, zwei oder drei schmale Goldstreifen; alle trugen den roten Stern der Republik auf der Kappenkrone. Rangabzeichen am Ärmel wie abgebildet -siehe englischen Bildtext für die einzelnen Ränge. J3 zeigt nach einem Foto eine nicht-reguläre Insignien-Anordnung auf dem Gorro. J4 & J5 zeigen die dreispitzigen Silberstern eines Divisions-oder Brigadekommandanten, getragen unterhalb der normalen Rangabzeichen; die Republik besaß nur einen Offizier im Generalsrang. J10 Ein typisches Rangabzeichen auf der Mütze eines Sergeanten.

K1 Dies ist spekulativ – nach bekannten, von anderen Brigaden verwendeten Mustern. K2 Nach einem Foto; eine Nachbildung ist erhalten geblieben. Die Fahne wurde bei Teruel an die Front getragen. K4 Nach Fotos; die Fahne wurde angefertigt, nachdem Clement Attlee, der spätere britische Premierminister, als Führer der Labourpartei diese Einheit besucht hatte.

L1 Nach einem Foto; die Farben der Fahne wurden gemäß den bekannten Farben der L2 MG-Kompanie des Bataillons bei Jarama angenommen. L3 Nach Fotos der ersten Gruppe und des letzteren Bataillons, das mit der 150. und 13. Brigade kämpfte. L4 Nach einem Foto; die Farben sind spekulativ.